ALSO BY SHEILA HETI

FICTION

Pure Colour

Motherhood

How Should a Person Be?

Ticknor

The Middle Stories

COLLABORATIONS

Women in Clothes

The Chairs Are Where the People Go

FOR CHILDREN

A Garden of Creatures

We Need a Horse

PLAYS

All Our Happy Days Are Stupid

ALPHABETICAL DIARIES

ALPHABETICAL

DIARIES

SHEILA HETI

FARRAR, STRAUS AND GIROUX

NEW YORK

Farrar, Straus and Giroux
120 Broadway, New York 10271

Library of Congress Cataloging-in-Publication Data
Names: Heti, Sheila, 1976– author.
Title: Alphabetical diaries / Sheila Heti.
Description: First edition. | New York: Farrar, Straus and Giroux, 2024.
Identifiers: LCCN 2023038965 | ISBN 9780374610784 (hardcover)
Subjects: LCSH: Heti, Sheila, 1976– | Literature, Experimental—
Canada. | LCGFT: Creative nonfiction. | Diaries.
Classification: LCC PR9199.4.H48 Z46 2024 | DDC 818/.607 [B]—
dc23/eng/20230828
LC record available at https://lccn.loc.gov/2023038965

Designed by Abby Kagan

Our books may be purchased in bulk for promotional, educational, or
business use. Please contact your local bookseller or the Macmillan Corporate
and Premium Sales Department at 1-800-221-7945, extension 5442, or by
email at MacmillanSpecialMarkets@macmillan.com.

www.fsgbooks.com
Follow us on social media at @fsgbooks

1   3   5   7   9   10   8   6   4   2

None of the characters in this book have their
literal analogues in the author's life.

ALPHABETICAL DIARIES

A book about how difficult it is to change, why we don't want to, and what is going on in our brain. A book can be about more than one thing, like a kaleidoscope, it can have many things that coalesce into one thing, different strands of a story, the attempt to do several, many, more than one thing at a time, since a book is kept together by its binding. A book like a shopping mart, all the selections. A book that does only one thing, one thing at a time. A book that even the hardest of men would read. A book that is a game. A budget will help you know where to go. A bunch of us met to have dinner that night, but I left and walked off by myself, bought the silver ring, a bag of chips, then sat in the main square and bummed a cigarette off an old French man, then continued to sit there for many hours until the man with the bulgy eyes came to sit next to me and flirt. A bus came which was going to the ferry, but because I hesitated before getting on, it drove angrily away. A certain kind of bore who has said all he is saying, said it all before, and expects to hear nothing new from you on the subject. A certain lack of self-centredness, belief in one's own innate genius, and faith in hard work, long hours. A child to love in that way, a man to want in that way, and all the collaborators; people with whom I can write the most heartbreaking books, and the books I write alone. A child until he is seven. A city in which people speak another language is good, because their conversations are not so distracting or irritating. A commitment to the relationship with the full understanding that the relationship will evolve and change as you two evolve and change. A curiosity about self-help. A desire to do acting. A desire to help people. A desire to uplift humanity. A different way of living now, according to my feelings and values, rather than according to stories and symbols. A drive to town for booze with Tom to get vodka for watching the movie. A fashion designer in *The New York Times Magazine* yesterday said, *I decided to be my homosexual self.* A feeling that he will completely reject me, that I don't know what's going on, or that he's mad. A feeling that I could occupy myself with this feeling forever. A feminist feeling. A few minutes later he returned and untied me. A few weeks ago there was a tick in my head, a kind of check mark—it happened in a dream and upon waking—about where I am in life, I had reached adulthood and the task would be different now. A few weeks ago, sleeping with him, I realized for the first time what it meant to have sex with somebody. A flush went up high in my cheeks. A funny thing happens with regards to men when one suddenly comes into a bit of money. A glamorous life I could be leading in New York, full of parties and glamorous people, never feeling sad, alone, left out, apart. A hot man who loves me. A human knows too little to answer such questions. A human must be responded to by a human. A husband is good insurance against the crazy, against the many things of the world. A Jane Austen novel, of course, or inspired by that. A kind of tyranny to think about beauty and love all the time, when there is really nothing to think about. A lack of values, a lack of privacy, and a lack of modesty, which is making me feel kind of sick. A life in a new place for a while. A life which is beside the main current of life. A little correspondence with Lemons. A little distance between this energy and myself. A little nervous. A little too long, and it's boring now. A look of concern, like my mother's look of concern, is settling over my face. A loss and an unhappiness. A lot of changes are happening. A lot of fear, but of what? A lot of people in their twenties get an addiction. A lot of talk about couples and dating, but the more I think about it, the more I think I've been in a pretty sweet situation this past month, not dating. A man must part company with the inferior and the superficial. A man of discretion. A man to love. A man who could physically kill me in under a minute is a man who is easy to sleep beside. A man who goes out in the world and gets what he wants for himself. A man who I could have in the centre of my life, even a child, and my family could fit themselves into the healthiness and happiness of that. A man who would be mine. A manic feeling yesterday made me almost rent out that apartment in New York, but I won't—it's not yet time for that. A mild form of hysteria, always. A moment after seeing him, a big lurch went through my stomach, and I tried not to look at him as we talked. A new relation to life. A new relationship, born from the ashes of the old and dead one. A new tone, a new ringtone. A nice kind of animal impulse to want to sit near a tree, just because it's a tree, and we continued to drink, from the blue goblet, the vodka and orange juice that Tom had squeezed with his bare hands. A person's life should not be so filled up that a surprise friend can't come in, but that doesn't mean they have to become your new best friend. A person's loyalty should always be to their partner, but I talked more than I wanted to or intended to about Pavel. A phone call from him yesterday—a surprise. A place I partly crave to settle into, but don't. A playfulness, a sense of life being without consequence, that voracious sexuality that wants to eat things

6

up, that selfishness, that kind of confidence and cockiness and ease, being on top of things, being in New York. A quiche and then an apple pie for dessert? A radical sympathy with all people based on their integrity as becomings, not beings; as people who experience the potential freedom of their own souls, so to radically know that people experience themselves from the inside, and not one person alive has ever experienced themselves from the outside. A return to writing. A ritual sacrifice of the purest animal I could find. A savory pie followed by a sweet pie? A series of titles? A shoddy world. A simple life, he would go home to have dinner with his wife and kids every night. A single life, good for so many of the phases and periods of life. A sudden happiness pierced me. A sweet kiss with him in front of the grocery store on Bloor, he kissed me on my cheek and I kissed him on the lips, just a sweet, little one. A tendency to idealize the past—that's me. A tremendous amount is lost when there's a break-up. A trip to L.A. A trip to New York. A wanderer on this tiny patch of earth. A waste of time, drinking. A white moth is resting on the windowsill. A woman and two men are travelling in the desert. A writer has to follow their curiosity, first and foremost. A writer is just one person under the stars, one person in a universe, writing about a whole entire universe. A young and attractive woman feels it should be otherwise, in her head. Ability to find monologue books. About decadence and narcissism. About humans in general. About leaving town. About to sell it soon, I think. Action in conformity with the situation. Activity and haste prevail. Actually, he doesn't love you. Actually, he doesn't want you. Actually, he is looking around the world for another girl, and because of who he is, he will find her and be with her. Actually, not that much is expected of you. Actually, people expect less of you than you think. Add that in as well. Added in about four thousand words, bringing it to 56,000. Advice from the old theatre director came in the form of *drop the word ex-girlfriend*, and Lars promised himself he would let himself be fucked if it would take him to two cities, London or New York. Affirmation can always be found from someone in any crowd, if that is what you are seeking. After all, I could only laugh at receiving that email from him, today in the courtyard, realizing I had chosen to forgo one man in Italy, only to return to two back home. After all, I never wanted anything to fall back on. After all, one does have to get back to work. After breaking up with him, I felt absolutely manic. After he left, I lay in bed, hungover, and the sun was shining into my room for the day. After hearing Agnes say that she is trying to stop crying, I think I might try that, too. After that, all I wanted was to play with my future children in a sun-dappled room. After that, I was in the shower, and I realized that despite the fact that the sex with Pavel had been bad, and I cried, I still felt happy. After that, I will have a clipping, and I will return to the agent I liked from the spring, and perhaps he can sell my story to *The New Yorker*, which will make me enough money to live there for seven or eight months. After that, invincibility. After the pool, we went into the shower and made out. After the show, I got drunk and did merch with Joseph. Afterwards, we all walked by the river. Agnes and I climbed the mountain and it was so intense up there on the lookout, crying and crying. Agnes has her jealousy, too. Agnes having a baby doesn't make me want to have a baby, but there is a way her life seems to move forward, everything around her always changing. Agnes is picking me up in an hour for her cottage. Agnes looked like a dignified woman suddenly, sort of neutered but still very pretty, and when a man our age came up, it turned out they knew each other because their children were friends, and she spoke of this connection with him in the way of a woman behind a wall, alluring but not meaning to be, but more alluring because she was behind a wall. Agnes said I would feel jealous for another fourteen months, and that she used to feel a lot of jealousy, too. Agnes said she doesn't think about breasts. Agnes said she had been crying all morning because she had left her daughter in day care for the first time, and she saw her daughter's face through the window, and her daughter had looked sad and confused. Agnes said she hadn't gone out with him because he wouldn't be a good provider. Agnes said she needed to be without her mother to grow up and feel able to be a mother herself. Agnes said she was taken in by her husband being handsome and manly; he was a doctor and charming and an intellectual who could talk about anything. Agnes said she wouldn't want to be with anyone but her husband because he is hard on her, calls her on things, and makes her a better person. Agnes said the most important thing is, *do you feel loved?* Agnes was so beautiful and pretty in her bikini, her body looked fabulous. Agnes who I love so much. Agnes who seems to have figured out everything before she was twenty-five. Agnes's life has so much integrity because around her is only what she wants and loves. Ah well. Ah well. Ah, who cares? Alice Munro's first book appeared when she was thirty-seven. All I am ambitious for is to publish this piece. All I can think about right now is fucking. All I ever wanted was to be an adult. All I ever wanted when I was younger was to be a writer, to be able to sit in one place and write things forever, and not feel like I had to do anything else. All I want are moments and more moments. All I want are some more experiences with him. All I want is to have breakfast with my friends, then to return home to this bright and beautiful sunny day. All I want is to read books for a year. All I want is to tell him that he should take care of himself, that he doesn't need to take care of me, that I can take care of myself, and that he ought to take care of himself first. All I wanted the next day was to get up and exercise, but when I woke, I was so tired from not sleeping the night before, that I did not. All I wanted was a physical life. All my faults are good for writing, what a strange thing. All my work is so pleasurable these days. All of a sudden he didn't seem very smart to me, and his belligerence wasn't very interesting, or his interest in gossip, or his vanity about being in New York and coming into contact with certain people, or his insistence on seeing me in a certain light. All of my twenties were so strange, all of life is so strange. All of them move forward in time and art without me. All of this is just the part of me which is my sexuality, which is why I have always wanted to escape it, why I have always wanted to be celibate. All of this must be doing something to me—to be devoted to him even in times of hardship and sore feelings. All of this seems key to the next part of life. All of this seems like the culmination of some searching in my life, but that's just the way I look at life, full of beginnings and endings. All of this will be impossible if I am with someone who makes it impossible. All of those projects seem dead, even the new novel seems dead, everything does. All of Toronto feels banal. All the elements of the world, everything I encounter and that other people encounter, can be put in a book. All the faith you had in art, you can have in this man. All the key players of my life are here, I feel. All the misery I always have when living with a man must not be some post-traumatic memory from the past visiting me, but something much more simple and mechanical, like that when I start living with someone, I start behaving in certain, patterned ways. All the people I hang out with who make me doubt, for various reasons and in various ways, my ability to keep a relationship going. All the people like Claire, for whom in their current relationship the sex is great. All the piles of dirt on the floor, waiting for me to collect them and put them away. All the really great things that have been created in art have been created by adults. All the time wondering what he's doing that makes it so he cannot write or call. All this morning, as I was cleaning up and wearing my green skirt, my thoughts kept thrusting Lars into my mind. All this should make me happy, but it's hard to relax. All this trip I had been trying to channel Simone de Beauvoir, thinking, *how would she behave on TV?* All this wandering about the world. All those weeks on tour, I felt consistently overtired, shaky and confused, and there was not one day when I did not fall asleep before the sky started to get light with morning. All we talk about is the way he wants to fuck me, and when he humiliated me last time, I felt flushed and angry, but then I liked him even more, even though I was ashamed to admit it—but it did turn me on, that he had the gall. All weekend, ever since he tied me up, my thumb has been buzzing with numbness. All white hair and so vibrant, a woman who knew what suited her—not a perfect life, but she got out of her marriage because it was not for her; she was not the marrying kind, she said. All you have wanted since you were twenty-five was to get back to that place of being seventeen, seeing friends who live close by, having sex, reading books and writing. All you want to do is go home, curl up and die. Almost collapsed writing that story. Alone in a room. Alone. Alone. Alone. Alone. Already I am feeling happier. Already I feel a spring of happiness inside me. Although what if living honestly doesn't get you where you want to go? Always feeling this tremble of insecurity and fear. Always having to smile and reassure everybody. Always I don't want to hurt the other person's feelings, so I act as pleasant as possible, meanwhile I am exhausted and getting a headache. Always the other is a source of strife in psychoanalysis. Always to be identifying the disease within ourselves. Always wanted to write a book that people would love. Always your books should be uninteresting. Am basically down to $0. Am checking email once a day and reading in the mornings. Am I going to finish cleaning the bedroom and the kitchen? Am I looking for love? Am I making the wrong decisions? Am I narrowing my life because of him, or just changing my priorities, and it's a bit messy, and it's going to be messy because I'm making new and different choices, which is what I want to do? Am I not being an artist now? Am I ready to give up my independent life? Am I saying that I'm marrying him now? Am I to spend the next day, two months, six months, however long, longing for Lars, hanging on his indifferent and careless emails, which he writes and sends and does not worry over? Am I wasting my time? Am low on money. Am making noodles. Am reading *Emma*. Am tired and will go to sleep. Am tired today and I feel like I may be getting a cold. Ambivalence gives you something to do, something to think about. Amelia has been working at the salon for fifteen years—since she was fifty-four. Amelia showed me how to shampoo, and I got water all over my skirt. Amelia would never ask a man to marry her, she said, turning away, and I felt really ashamed. Among other things we said to each other yesterday was that when I said I wouldn't cheat on him, Pavel said I couldn't cheat on him because if another man's dick got within one inch of my vagina, the relationship was over. An email from Lemons today about love and friendship and attraction that said nothing. An ideal life would be to have several boyfriends or husbands at once. An inability to work as much as the energy inside me allows. An interest in a wide variety of people. An interest in doing research. An interest in sex. An interest in streetcar drivers. And already it has lost its charm. And as for Lemons, I feel deadly uninterested in being his friend or confiding in him ever. And at a certain point I will grow tired of writing like this, and that will be the end of mapping my insides. And basically the culture wants us not to grow up so we're like this all our lives. And cleaning the apartment was like cleaning up shop. And coffee. And *Crime and Punishment*, for sure. And don't think anymore about cocks going in and out. And don't use the word *sweetheart* with Pavel, whose name you still have to search for sometimes. And earlier, wondering what is wrong with me that I didn't give him a chance last summer, but by the end of the night remembering, for to have to hear him talk all the time, I would always be wanting him out of my apartment. And everything he said in his last letter was sincere. And everything I eat tastes like hospital food. And everything I know about a human life. And falling into men. And for God's sake, stop telling people like Lemons and Fiona about my relationship problems! And hard, dishonest, claustrophobic and destined to doom as soon as I moved in with him. And he denies this, but I remember clearly that he said that I would meet the man of my dreams when I was thirty, and then I would stop writing. And here he was, so beautiful—more beautiful than in my memory of him, even the waitress couldn't keep her eyes off him, or the man who was sitting at the bar, but Lars is so pretty that he doesn't notice any of this. And how he looked at dinner, while we were talking. And how I am drawn to addicts. And how I am drawn to love like an addiction. And how I am happy about that. And how I am not sleeping enough. And how I am not working right now. And how I am working too hard. And how it was positioned inside me. And how little he understands about how much I feel for him. And how much that makes me want him! And I became happy. And I became very happy all of a sudden. And I cooked all day, first the carrots, then the fresh pesto I had picked up from the market. And I didn't want to tell him about my day. And I didn't. And I do have a feeling that he wants to destroy strong women, as he once said. And I imagined him with a wedding ring on his finger, and I suddenly got wet. And so the struggle will continue. And then he and I went to his apartment and fought and yelled at each other all night. And then talking to Rosa about him today, she pointed out that he has never treated me as someone he wants to have a relationship with, but as someone he's really fond of that he likes fucking. And there is nothing more complicated to it than that. And there is nothing weak about this. And to know what humans are. And to live aloneish. And what is a bad person anyway? And you do things that are punishments to yourself, or things that harm you, or that are self-inflicted pain. Anyway, I am not crying about him, though several days ago I was. Anyway, later he cut a piece of bread for me. Anyway, who knows? Are we cowards if we choose the lesser honour? Are you going to war or are you drawing in an audience? Art changes the opinion of the masses, as much as science does. Art in other cultures, in cultures that were more concerned about the well-being of the group, had art that was not so concerned with inner psychology and one's isolated problems, but problems as they affected the tribe. Art is not essential, but love is essential, and maybe that is why people make art, to express their love of something—that tree, humans, the world, language, intensity of thought—and the person who doesn't respond to a work of art is perhaps missing the love of the thing which the artist is pointing to, lovingly. Art is too much a tool for ambition, and not even the ambition to make something beautiful—which, as I write it, seems exhausting, too—but just the personal ambition to rise above other people. Art, I saw yesterday, is not a benign or pleasant, do-goodery thing to be doing, I don't know how I hadn't seen it before. As Claire dashes from the world of filmmaking, and Hanif dashes from the world of literature, and Pavel, who has never had a world, simply dashes about. As I write it, I know that this is just a moment of high confidence which will certainly pass. As if I could go down into the lobby and fuck anyone I found there. As Rosa said, *it only takes an afternoon to get pregnant*. As we approached the field from the forest. As we walked to the hotel through the street. As well, I was talking about the sadness of being oneself. Aside from that, life is really good right now. At last, the ambassador's wife came over, and she was like a second-rate first lady, and she had a very earnest way about her, and she spoke to the young man about how good it was for him to be in the foreign service, and he replied that after September 11th, it was the only thing he wanted to do, and she said that she was looking for some young genius to help her—and he perked up—and she said, *to help me with my computer*. At one point Fiona was like, *you're such a good listener*. At one point Rosa was talking about how she didn't like New York literary parties, because it was all forty-year-old men hitting on women in their twenties, and I turned to Lemons and said, *it's terrible, do you understand this?* and he gave me a sweet smile with a twist in his mouth. At one point Tom said, *this was Ted*

Hughes's room. At the beginning of the night, people were mostly talking with the people they came to the party with. At the end of the night, Lemons said, *well anyway, I just wanted to tell you about my dilemma,* but it wasn't a dilemma at all.

B ack at his place, he showed me pictures of his ex-girlfriend, and I talked to him about Lars. Back home, I just lay in my room alone and masturbated, content with my mediocrity. Bad metaphor, humans as machines. Bah. Bakery in Berlin. Basically it's a crazy year, that's what Claire said, this is going to be a crazy year. *Be a pro*, Lemons said. Be a woman. *Be an individual*, he suggested. Be bald-faced and strange. Be calm. Be cautious with your money. Be clean and attractive. Be comfortable and assured and confident in your work life. *Be creative*, is what Pavel thinks people are told, and what is expected of a person, now more than ever. Be direct about the things you need that are reasonable requests, and apart from that, just enjoy him and your time together. Be impeccable with your word. Be miserable about the world. Be optimistic, for you know how steady application always gets you somewhere.

Be patient and hold on to your vision and integrity. Be peaceful, do little, find the one good thing, the one solace in the moment. Be thoughtful and wise. Be very quiet, very humble, very grateful. Be worse than you were when you were younger, and allow that to be a fact, that people around you will interact with less than common grace and decency, they will interrupt and disappoint one another, and they will not always behave as you would want—in that good way. Because another person is not a tool for your own self-development. Because as Claire was saying the other night, one's thoughts are always changing. Because *beauty* is a word reserved for art, and I'm not sure to what degree to consider this new book art. Because by the time I reach the computer to write, I've so exhausted my mind that the only thing I have the energy for is answering emails. Because for so long I've wondered if I'm not heartless to always be breaking up with men, or thinking about breaking up, but what if it's something else—what if it's a neurotic need to repeat the insecure feeling of things coming to an end? Because I am in debt and don't know how I'm going to live. Because I am not writing. Because I am sad. Because I am with a man. Because I couldn't leave, I tried to find the dinner party interesting, but I was unable to find anything interesting about Lemons's new girlfriend. Because I had love until this weekend, I didn't think money was important.

Because I had sex with Lars. Because I have zero dollars. Because I will probably ruin my life. Because I would get bored. Because I would leave. Because it is a pattern, and the pattern is: be with me, desire Laurel; be with Laurel, desire me. Because it would be better to write one really good story, like *Frankenstein* or something, just once, it doesn't have to be more than once, just come up with a really good story, probably a tragedy. Because it's emotion that makes something compelling, and I don't know to what extent to consider this new book emotional. Because it's the whole truth. Because Lars seems not neurotic, I feel like the things I do that might wound another man would drop off him. Because one is always falling in high heels, falling forwards. Because that's the sort of woman he wants, and that's not me. Because the money isn't here for nail polish, or lipsticks, so now that you have nail polish, now that you have lipsticks, now that you have this green skirt about which Pavel said, *keep it on*, then proceeded to fuck you in, stop spending money on such junk. Because the standards here are so low, my standards have also become low. Because there is no God to ask forgiveness from if we trespass religious laws, we must ask for forgiveness from each other for trespassing or failing to honour human laws. Been thinking about authenticity, and about how we have been done a great disservice by being taught that what we are to be authentic to is our feelings, as opposed to our values. Before falling asleep, I was thinking about my fundamental insecurity in the world, and I wondered if it was possible for me to feel safe even for one minute. Before I boarded the plane, they made us sit for a long time in the suffocatingly hot bus. Before speaking to Rosa, I was reading a Leonard Cohen interview, and he said that the longer he lived, the more he understood that he was not in charge. Being a lazy wanderer with no mission is definitely an option. Being back in Toronto brought close the truth of how I felt being onstage with the band those two weeks, which was: very bad. Being high for the first time on tour, I saw how amazing it all was, how remarkable and new, and how interesting all these people I was travelling with were. Being onstage in front of a crowd that is screaming for you and applauding your name—this is not an experience I feel I need. Besides, there is nothing wrong with writing books that come out of an inner security, peace, watching, reflection. Best not to get too rosy-eyed about each other, so that when I return to him, we aren't disappointed. Best not to live too emotionally in the future—it hardly ever comes to pass. Better to be on the outside, where you have always been, all your life, even in school, nothing changes. Better to look outward than inward. Blow jobs and tenderness. Books that fall in between the cracks of all aspects of the human endeavour. Books that would express this new philosophy, this somehow post-capitalist philosophy, or whatever it would be that could say, in the worldly sense, *be a loser*, and not with the religious faith that you will be rewarded for it later. Both of them were in important relationships, then they had a passionate affair, and now they're suddenly together. Both those meetings, though good for my books and my work, did not feel good for my soul or for my moral progress in the world. Bought a good spray for getting out stains because my overcoat had gotten stained with wine the night before, then I hung around on Adam Phillips's tidy London street and bought some hair elastics and arrived at his house a bit early. Bought a lot of clothes, make-up, spent a lot of money. Bought tea. Bought white shoes. Brunch with friends this weekend? Brunch with Lemons and Ida. Build a life together, step by step. Building a fireplace and being cozy. But after getting out of the car tonight, I realized that actually, with writing, I have something far more valuable than money. But also, there is no Platonic world. But any change is really hard and a real risk because it means not controlling the outcome; it means you don't know where you're going to end up, so if you're at all determined to get somewhere—to some fixed spot in the future—it's hard to let yourself change. But as I was saying this, I was realizing that my feeling about it was changing, and I saw that there was something fascinating about living only one life, and in some ways there is a great privilege in getting to live only one life and not having to live any others. But I had some good pierogis anyway. But I just wanted to mark down that I am happy. But I mostly don't feel like I can spend much time with Pavel anymore, for he irritates me on a very deep level. But love can endure. But love is not enough. But love without compatibility is a constant pain. But my task is not to love him, but simply to love—to be a person who loves—so to love him as part of an overall loving, not at the exclusion of everyone else, with blinders on, focused only on him, but rather focused on the entire universe, for the universe is my first relationship, the fundamental one; then beyond that, to love all of creation, which includes the man I am with. But of course it was a joke. But the essential thing is to remain persevering in order not to deviate from the right path. But then I left and bought myself a round of cheese from the grocery store, and a Minute Maid and a bottle of water and some bread from the bakery—it was delicious—and I was so hungry that I drank the juice as soon as I got outside and I immediately felt better; but before, sitting in the restaurant when the woman wouldn't take my order and kept laying out knives, I had never been so irritable. But then I started to cry because I didn't want to start things up with him again. But this morning I am not worried about it, I do not care. Buy food with Mom. Buying skin cream. By staying here, my world closes in. By the end, people around you will be dying off, and they will be thinking about their own deaths and the deaths of their partners so entirely that they won't have time to notice what you have accomplished, or how you managed to live such a faultless life, they're just going to be thinking about how their wife is dying, or how their husband has died, or about how there's nobody in the world who will love them as much or understand them so well, while you will be sitting here all alone with your great pride over the life you have crafted, and the work you have made, and everything you did to make yourself so perfect and good. By which I mean, not having children, being with the wrong man, having no love in the end, and being sort of penniless and maybe ignored.

Calculate your money and move forward. Call Fiona. Call her and see how she's doing. Called Fiona. Calling up bad memories reinforces them to the exclusion of the good ones and turns the good ones bad. Came back here and worked and worked. Can I be happy in this way? Can I be truthful? Can I believe that things will turn out well when he and I are reunited? Can I withstand the storm in him and myself, the fear that rises and says, *do not stay!* Can we wait until New Year's Eve or should we start it up right away? Can you take life seriously and exhibit in yourself the characteristics you most admire about him—that is, make your brain think about the things you value and find most interesting to think about, just control your brain, which in my case means not thinking about men and love and sex so much, or about seduction and beauty, but instead about art and how the next book should be and other aspects of the world, like how we all relate, without having it always come back to yourself? Can't be avoided. Cancel Barcelona, you don't have to travel unnecessarily. Cancel with Pavel and do nothing for the rest of the week but work, apart from depositing the cheque, sending in the invoice, asking about the contract, letting Lemons know that a new draft is coming, sending out emails, getting a haircut. Cancelled New Year's with Rosa. Cancelled with Pavel. Cause I really have been thinking about it and realizing that this is what I always do: move in with someone and almost instantly get depressed. Cause I'll leave. Cause I'm selfish. Cause there is no evading it anymore. Causing pain to others is part of being in this machine, in this human body. Changing your view on this is like trying to imagine, on the subway, that you are hurtling east, not west. Check with the world, like when you next talk to Lars, ask him why he didn't write you back, and tell him how it made you feel. Checked my email. Checking my email felt so vomitous. Choose men independent of any concerns, apart from, *is this someone I want to share my heart and my body and my friends and my family with?* Choose men independent of what they might or might not do for my work. Claire hated the stuff she saw at all the galleries she went to, all but three paintings at MoMA. Claire is a great artist. Claire is able to ride this so well, to not reveal any bad or negative feelings, and to be bright and unsuspicious when interviewed, to lean up close and to seem to be having a good time. Claire is an entertainer and a politician, but she is not actually an artist. Claire is made for this role and is not fucking it up. Claire is smart about so much stuff, but she is not so smart about other people's feelings. Claire is so in touch with her audience, is such a good and funny person, and is so intelligent and learned and tall. Claire just gave me a ton of her clothes. Claire looked beautiful, her skin was so amazingly clear. Claire offered me her Brooklyn apartment for two weeks, but no part of me feels like going. Claire said a therapist told her to shun intrigue, so now when she has a crush, she *tells* her boyfriend, rather than hiding it from him like she used to. Claire said she didn't want to be like an actress or someone who gets famous and suddenly publishes a book, but she really had been working on this book of six stories, and wanted to one day publish it. Claire said she thought the greatest thing in the world was to write a novel. Claire said she totally recognized the feeling, she called it a panic attack, and I said I still have them, and she said she does, too, and I said, *it's a kind of trilling in my chest*, and I said I'd felt it earlier in the day, and she said she had, too, and she asked me, *what do you do about it?* and I said, *I don't do anything about it.* Claire said she would only want to read a story by me from St. Petersburg if I killed myself in the end. Claire said that it's good for an artist to be in a relationship with someone who gets them out of their head. Claire said that love has never been a problem for her. Claire said that most men want a simple woman, but that some have a taste for complex women, like her own boyfriend. Claire spoke about Joan Didion, and how annoyed she felt at the tiny bites of toast she took at the party, with all these guys hanging around her, and last night I had a dream where I kept licking my lips and was parched for water and I kept touching my mouth, and Joan Didion was like, *can you not do that?* Claire thinks I should write every day, and I probably should, even though I never have, at least not fiction. Claire was comparing casual sex to cigarettes, saying that the craving is gone in the morning. Claire's boyfriend has taken a lover, and she says she has never felt such trust before, more than in any of her previous relationships. Claire's choices in life are like strokes on a canvas, decisive. Claire's light just gets brighter and brighter, and bigger and bigger; she's not a misanthrope, that's why. Clean out closets. Cleaning, throwing things out, especially from the stairwell, going to the store and finding something nice for the kitchen, then hauling the washer into the street. Clothes: don't buy anything over $100. Coffee tomorrow morning! Collaborating to no end no longer has the allure it had two weeks ago. Collect boxes. Come back down to earth. Come down to earth and understand that Lars has rejected you and will not want you ever. Coming back from the bathroom, I really wanted to ask Claire how beautiful or not she thought I was; how she estimated my looks. Coming home from the hospital, I lay in Trinity Bellwoods Park for an hour. Coming out of the metro with Amandine on my way to the embassy, I had my first glance of the Eiffel Tower, and I couldn't believe it was in the same place I was. Commitment, then freedom from within what one has committed to. Communicate with others as clearly as you can to avoid misunderstandings, sadness, drama. Compatibility, I think, matters more than love. Complaining about your relationship with Pavel—ridiculous; don't try to gain attention from the world the way you did in the seventh grade, when the teachers asked everyone if the older kids gave us alcohol at the cast party, and you lied and said yes. Conquering the world doesn't mean as much as it used to, but, as Hanif says, one still has to work. Conserve your energies. Control negative thinking. Count your money and see how you're doing. Crazy to spend ninety dollars on the scarf—but I'm crazy! Create the fiction. Crushes on men. Crying about Lars. Curiosity is not a good reason to get married.

Dad just now told me that my twenties were for experimentation and playing around, but now that I'm thirty, I should settle down and focus on my work; that this is the time to see what I can achieve. Dad read an earlier draft and had some suggestions about how to make it more real, but I don't think I want it to be too real. Dad said that none of the younger doctors had any authority, and that what he wanted was for somebody to tell him what to do, to just lay it out exactly. Dad said this morning that my work was the most important thing since my relationships seem to come and go. Dad says not to analyze things so much, but what should I do with all my bad feelings and fears? Dad told me that his plan, if they were going to keep him past Tuesday, would be to put on his clothes, leave the hospital, get a cab, have the cab drop him off at the base of the bridge on Bathurst, and throw himself off. Dad was perhaps a little manic, the doctors having started him on steroids again. Dad was upset today when the nurse said that what he needed was calories. Dad went home from the hospital today. Dad's wrists were so skinny, thin and weak, and he said it was because the platelets were gone from all his operations and illness. Dante's *Inferno*. Dating is terrible. Daydreaming like this, I fell off my bike on Shaw, missing a dip in the road and losing control of the bike, and smashed up my knee. Deep in the field a boy and girl came up and sat with us. DFW died. Did I betray him? Did I? Did not get much writing done, obviously. Didn't sleep at all last night, and feel unable to sleep right now. Difficult evening last night. Difficult men. Disappointed a bit, but fine. Discipline like discipleship. Discretion is part of it. Do away with the idea, the romantic idea, of essence. Do I hold myself back from fear of surpassing him? Do I want to be his primary partner? Do I want to be in a sexless relationship? Do I want to grow old with this man? Do not introspect. Do nothing but accept who you are. Do that instead of escaping into fantasies of lives with other men, men who I have already made the conscious choice of rejecting. Do we have to suffer until the end of history? Does he die, drowning, trying to kiss himself? Does he stare forever at his image? Does it create distance between you and the man that you're with? Does it deserve forgiveness? Does it get you closer to any particular man? Does it get you closer to men in general? Does it get you closer to wisdom? Does it get you closer to your truest values? Does it have a positive effect? Does it throw a wrench in the wheel? Does one live in expectation of roses and a country home? Does that lead to poverty, to trials, to love? Does the city make me this way, or age, or finishing a book that I think is no good? *Does the imagination work that fast?* Pavel asked. Don't affect this cool air, this worldly air. Don't anticipate the worst, always fearing it. Don't ask the question *why*, *why* are you writing this? Don't ask too much of yourself on this trip, just try to get some work done, see a few paintings, and find a hotel with as little fuss and bother as possible. Don't be afraid of becoming more conscious and more aware—you can't stay unconscious, you must use as much of your brain as possible; besides, if there isn't an unconscious, you're doing yourself a disservice by not thinking. Don't be afraid of not having money come. Don't be covetous. Don't be fatalistic. Don't be frivolous. Don't be miserable. Don't be scared. Don't be so impressed with yourself, but do the good work. Don't become like the pathologists, thinking you've seen the insides of people, and that the outside's prettier. Don't check your email in the mornings or do any other work in the morning apart from typewriter work. Don't commit to anything. Don't confess or complain. Don't contribute to any project unless you're genuinely excited about it. Don't delude yourself. Don't demand, but take care of yourself, see your friends, make plans, go out. Don't do blurbs next year if you can help it. Don't do readings. Don't do so many interviews, don't take on any new assignments, just figure out money and plan financially for the next few years. Don't end up in Paris, end up somewhere cheap. Don't evoke by magic, but do the thinking, do the work. Don't expect big things from yourself in the near term. Don't feel like talking to Fiona tonight. Don't feel obliged to do anything. Don't feel pressure from people who work at the magazines. Don't forget how hard all this is, how hard it is for him, how hard it is for everyone. Don't forget that although you aren't telling a story, you must still do what stories do, which is lead the reader through an experience. Don't forget that the book will exist in the future. Don't forget to write, even if it's going nowhere. Don't forget to write, even though it will never be published. Don't forget—they project onto you their unfulfilled needs. Don't get into relationships with men you want to fuck—just fuck them. Don't get pulled into the shallowness of it all. Don't hold on to the past. Don't let your ego and ambition make you desire power over other people, but do whatever you can to avoid that. Don't let your life become a fiction. Don't make up stories. Don't make yourself a god. Don't make yourself into a demon. Don't pull the reader along. Don't read just to strengthen your own point of view. Don't remain ignorant just to preserve the simplicity of your own point of view. Don't see too many people in New York. Don't spend so much money. Don't spend so much time on Twitter or Facebook or in correspondence or getting involved in other people's art projects. Don't take anything personally. Don't take yourself so seriously; don't think about yourself at all. Don't teach or do residencies. Don't think about celibacy. Don't think about dating or alternate ways you can make money. Don't think about sleeping with Lars, it's only making you anxious. Don't think about the structure in terms of morality, good or evil, what should or shouldn't be. Don't think in terms of great art or great artist; think in terms of the work. Don't think of yourself as a woman while writing it—don't think of yourself at all, don't come back to your own experiences; it's okay if it contradicts your experience of life. Don't train yourself to be cold, but it's not so bad to have some control over yourself. Don't underestimate what people see; they see hearts, it's clear to everyone. Don't want to be killed, but if I am, it's no great tragedy, and there's no dignity in worrying about it. Don't waste your energies on doubt over everything. Don't worry about L.A. Don't worry about New

York. Don't worry about whether Lars will show anyone the naked pictures you sent him, you can't do anything about it now. Done, done, done. Dream of me yelling at my mother, *nothing I did was ever good enough for you!* Dresden. Drinking a lot. Drinking and smoking, to some extent, help.

arlier in the day, we fucked. Earlier in the day, we talked about feminism, and about how can anyone not be a feminist? Earlier in the day, when we were sitting on the concrete slab, Lemons said his greatest wish in life was to marry a woman and to have no doubts about her in his mind. Earlier, I got mad at him that I had talked with him about his book for an hour, and he could not ask a single question of me. Earlier, I walked with Piper all the way up to the plateau, and we talked about our next projects, which felt very fated because she had been there at the dawn of the last one; I had conceived of it when I was nervously up at her island cottage, with her friends who I did not know. Earlier, in another German town, I had stolen some little ice cream squares, then smoked a cigarette on the tiny carousel, then Joseph got on, then Jack got on, then we got off so some teenagers could get on. Eat better and better all the time. Eating a donut. Eating, don't put anything inside you that you don't think should be there. Edmund White said, *I invited Ellis because he's so cute and interesting, and he invited you!* Edmund White seemed to take everyone on par, even though at the end of the night he called me *Shelly*. Either because I'm a bad person and he can see it, or because he's a bad person. Either way is depressing right now. Ellis had a beautiful hotel room and we drank white wine and ordered room service and talked. Ellis met me at the door as I was coming out, and was very warm immediately. Ellis said nobody should attribute classiness to any of his actions, that he hoped no one would, and that the reason he didn't order dessert was because he had not been very hungry. Ellis showed me how in his bag there was just his *Austerlitz*, a water bottle and a single piece of paper—it was lined and folded in half. Ellis talked about democracy and the two books he wanted to write. Ellis told himself, *if I don't find my* Austerlitz, *I will never write again.* Ellis took me to Laurel's concert—very beautiful and simple piano compositions. Empty out drawers, cupboards, the side stairwell, clothes you don't like, won't wear. Enough of the book is invented, isn't it? Enough of this. Enough. Equivocal or vague principles, as a rule, will make your life an undirected, uninspired and meaningless act. Especially if I were a man. Especially when I first meet someone. Especially with my hair pulled back in a hairband like this. Essentially I explained to Rosa that I was hiding my sensitivity from him because I was afraid that this part of myself would scare him and then he wouldn't love me, and she said my sensitiveness was part of who I am, and who I am is beautiful, and if I wasn't sensitive I wouldn't be a writer, and that I had to communicate this to him and share all of myself with him or else it wouldn't work. Even as I write this, I know I'm not as intelligent as the most intelligent ones. Even as much as I truly adore Pavel and my heart leans towards him, there is some part of me that feels like I would be settling for a relationship I wouldn't want to be in. Even if he is, on some level, a person I would enjoy being with, on a whole other level, he is the most untrustworthy person I have ever met, and better that I am bitterly disappointed now than when I'm forty. Even if he makes you feel ashamed, that's better than feeling nothing. Even if he's right, that we should only meet once in a while and do what he says we do best—fuck—I know my feelings, and if I've learned a few things, one of them is that everything will be the same the second time around. Even if I'm stronger, that's not necessarily better for someone like me, who perhaps should not always be so strong. Even if it

turns out you misplaced your faith, have faith. Even if someone doesn't turn you on, if they do it right, it can turn you
on. Even if the relationship makes me unhappy and lonely
and alienated and upset—stay. Even last night as we talked
about his money problems and his fears for his future, I felt
my hands and feet tingling. Even more to the point, Em-
manuel Bove, Wallace Shawn, Gerhard Richter, Jane Bowles,
Paul Bowles. Even more to the point, Manet. Even walking
to the Shoppers Drug Mart, I started to exhaust myself totally. Even with Lars I would experience restlessness. Even
with Vig there is that danger. Eventually I might grow tired
of the effort, like the Mishima character, but this is another
good thing about reading—one replaces thinking about one's
self and life with thinking about the selves and lives of
fictional people. Eventually this jealousy will fade, I hope.
Every bell sounds two ways, coming and going. Every choice
is a risk. Every day I should make myself the goal of not
being needy, and keep in mind that horrible girl on the
plane. Every man must have something he follows. Every
once in a while it's good to leave your home. Every person
has to figure themselves out on their own. Every time I am
happy, I fear I must be delusional, and that I'm only happy
because there is a major part of the truth of the situation
that I'm missing, and it is this fundamental and eclipsing

denial that is making me happy. Every time I ask for advice, I feel worse, so I will ask for no more advice. Every time I look up, the sky changes colour; now everything is dark and in shadows. Every time we have sex it feels different, and he kept his fingers inside me for a while after he made me cum and said that my pussy felt so great that night, tight and soft and warm, which isn't a way he has talked to me in a long time. Everyone feels bad, everything was ruined, but what if something was also created? Everyone loads the gear into the van, the bigger and heavier things first, then unloads them at the club. Everyone said how good we looked together. Everyone telling me these days that I look so good. Everything has to be sacrificed for writing. Everything I have done in the last while I have done with Lars in mind—dancing, painting the hall, cleaning out the stairwell. Everything is more beautiful and glittering in my mind than it ever is in real life. Everything is very close right now, is about to be brought into being, is just millimeters away. Everything kept neat; there is marmalade on toast. Everything should be very easy right now. Everything was fine until I texted him last night and the tally came to three from me and two from him. Everything with me goes nowhere. Everything you are doing since you left for New York to meet with Lemons has been a total mess. Everything. Exactly one year ago today I was on my first date with Fiona, fooling around and I guess having sex with her on the living room rug. Exhausting to think about all that now when I am already feeling so exhausted.

F ear at base. Fear of not being able to justify myself, or of not being productive every moment of the day; an inferiority complex that manifests itself in the sense that I must always be justifying my existence by thinking. Feel like there is something else I should be working on. Feeling an inability to work as much as the energy inside me allows. Feeling anxious these past few days, in part because of Pavel talking about moving in together, and in part for reasons I do not know. Feeling overwhelmed and bad. Feeling very anxious and depressed, like I wanted to cry all day, and I couldn't remember how long I'd felt this way for. Feeling your personality infusing and soaking into everything you do—this contributes to a lack of charm in life. Feelings aren't a choice. Feelings aren't the most important thing, but rather doing the important things that need doing, but all of that is thrown to the wind when I'm in a bad mood. Felt a bit like my mother last night. Felt pretty happy after my revelation on Friday that I wasn't doomed to be in bad relationships because of some magical thing, like the memory of being in a family. Fiction and nonfiction together, because the imagination is more amazing than anything in life, and life is more amazing than anything you can make up. Fiction is a small, very small part of what preoccupies me. Fiddling as Rome burns. Figure out money transfer. Figure out what the next book will be. File my taxes—important. Finally he took off his underwear and I held his balls as he went to sleep. Finally he was turned away from me on the pillow, and I said I wanted to see his beautiful face, and when he turned back around, he had set his mouth strangely open with his tongue hanging out, and he bobbled his head around, and his eyelids were turned inside out—yellow and shiny and pink and disgusting. Finally I have broken up with Pavel, which I have wanted to do for so long. Find women. Fine detailed work, gradations of truth, starting from scratch, not from ideology but from lives, and moving outward from there. Finish the book since it is finished with me. Finish the book, send it to Lemons, get some money for it. Finish the *Esquire* piece. Finish two books and begin a third, then finally enrol in hairdressing school. Finished my book the day before yesterday, and I told myself I'd not turn on my computer until tomorrow, but yesterday I got up wanting to write. Finishing something will make it good. Fiona and I talked about old relationships and—I don't even remember what! Fiona asked me the name of my bunny and cat. Fiona bought herself a little tiger that looked like the one from her dream. Fiona didn't feel loved by her ex-girlfriend. Fiona gave me a pink jewel to remind me of the pink shoes I didn't buy. Fiona got dressed and we went to have breakfast at the place we had eaten at the day before. Fiona has a nervous habit of moving her lips in a way that is like a baby suckling. Fiona has spent the past two days cleaning her apartment and looking through mementos. Fiona is moving to Australia with her new boyfriend. Fiona is very interesting, but of course she sometimes irritates and bores me, that's just the way people are. Fiona lay down on the bed and went to sleep. Fiona looked exhausted and sad. Fiona never dates men. Fiona once said that the point is not only to be around each other on good days—when we're feeling happy—but whenever, even when we're feeling bad. Fiona said nobody could promise not to change. Fiona said she wanted me to know that she was with me, that she would not leave me, and that she meant it when she said she wanted to build a life together. Fiona was stroking me and I had a white tank top on. Fiona works at an abortion clinic where there are regularly women in their forties coming in. For Ellis, the source of guilt is telling his own story; that the contemporary white male American novelist does not feel he owns his experiences sufficiently, or if he owns them they do not matter—they are not the important stories to be told. For Hanif, the problem is our place in literary history, post-Beckett, who starved the novel of setting and self, so setting and self must be self-consciously and deliberately won. For instance, I believed that Ellis didn't order dessert out of a kind of good breeding—that because he had not been invited to dinner, but was a tagalong like me, he didn't want to overtax his welcome, so I condemned myself for ordering dessert, for being such a boor. For instance, one could use words like *sublimely controlled*, *masterful*, *impactful*, *transformative*, or whatever. For my soul had been sucked out of me from all that fighting. For some reason, I had the feeling that is so common with me, that I have ruined everything, or that everything was ruined. For some reason, I told Lemons the story about being so in love with Gil in high school, then sleeping with him a year ago, then the whole thing that happened with me missing our high school reunion and him calling me the next day and asking where I'd been, and I was saying to Lemons how it's funny that whenever you get the things you want, it's never when you wanted them, or in the form in which you imagined you'd get them, and he said, *yes, it's like there's some metaphysical law that a desperate want for something results in the withholding of that thing.* For

47

some reason, when I think of this, I feel happy. For sure I can see the risk with Lars, that he might not be able to stay with me as he couldn't with the other girls, but if I look down deeper, to what is deepest, I believe we can bring it off if I can stay true in my heart to what I want. For the first day here, I was miserable and utterly wanted to die, then I was almost ecstatic, then just as quickly, my life felt cluttered with people. For the most part, I cannot deny certain feelings, and I cannot pretend I have other ones. For the most part, I like the way I live and mostly want to continue living this way, even if it's not so big, glamorous, exciting or interesting, and even if very little changes as the years go by. For the next hour or two, I don't even know what happened—I avoided them as best I could, and spoke to various other people, took a walk in the garden and finally left and went to the journalists' dinner, which was where I ate my first meal of the day at around ten o'clock at night, but by mistake I ordered the bouillabaisse instead of the meat, so Hanif, who was sitting next to me, gave me some of his chicken, as did the interviewer I remembered from February. For the second time in two days, Claire told me the story of being overawed by her mother, who, as an old woman, told her that she felt she'd wasted too much of her life being nice to other people. For there is only one pleasure that doesn't fade, and that's not love—that's art. For this, I need new clothes.

Forced myself to wake up early. Forced myself to write five thousand words today, and saw that, even with the distractions of last night, I could do it, and was glad. Forget about characters. Forget about Lars. Forget about the email to Pavel, it doesn't matter. Forgetting that I have a life apart from him, value apart from him, and can take care of myself apart from him; that I am as valuable as anybody else in this world, and that he isn't more valuable than me. Friendship is more stable anyway. From now on, when I'm feeling like I did yesterday—so lost, so restless—I can just come to my desk. Fuck, Lars is gorgeous. Fucking him all last year. Fucking someone solves nothing. Funny how I didn't see this at the time.

Gazing down at him with his eyes closed, I thought, *I do not love this man*. Gertrude Stein was in her thirties when she met Alice and Picasso. Get a lot of money and move on. Get a new computer for your efforts. Get a new set of dressers for my clothes and linens. Get a new tape recorder that is digital, and maybe get a foot pedal for transcribing. Get a new typewriter or find your old one. Get a passport, do it next week. Get *Death in Venice*. Get money from wherever you can. Get off the pill. Get paid. Get started on it again. Get started on your next project. Getting back together with Lars felt so natural, so easy. Getting high with her always ends up strengthening my conviction that confidence is what's needed. Getting out of the car tonight, I realized that, actually, with writing, I have something far more valuable than money. Gil asked me if I wanted my book to be talked about by young people in coffee shops. Gil bought himself a few acres of land, I don't know how he was able to afford it. Gil is so sexy. Gin and tonic with lemon or lime. Giovanna has been sick. Giovanna has her writers in tears. Giovanna is in her mid- to late sixties. Giovanna is not what people make her out to be; she doesn't seem intimidating or to hate all women, and I find her quite vulnerable, though she doesn't listen so well, it's true. Giovanna seemed pleased to see me, and smiled in such a genuine and generous way, though a little ironically. Giovanna seems to like me and to direct most of her conversation towards me. Giovanna told the story about me that when I arrived at the residency, I announced to her that I had just fallen in love, so I didn't know about writing, then I left early for love as well. Giovanna was ignoring me and trying to win the other writers to her side. Give the reader everything, which is the opposite of the modernist thing of expecting the reader to put it all together, to fill in the gaps. Gives me vertigo just to think about it. Go back to the summer when you were seventeen. Go home and look at your money, at what has come in. Go to sleep. Go to stranger areas of the city to get lost in and read. Going back to Toronto, it will be cold. Going out in my shorts, even though it's November. Going to Chicago on the eve of Obama's election. Going to glamorous parties at least sometimes. Going to New York to work with Lemons. Good book

51

thinking done today. Good editing skills. Good for nothing but publicity. Got a very funny email from Dave Hickey last night—I wrote him saying, *love from Dave is even better than working at a university*, and he wrote back saying, *and it doesn't last as long*. Got in a cab and took it to Le Poisson Rouge. Got the purple jacket. Got to the airport; they scanned the bags and checked through the luggage three times. Grandma died. Grandma has been sick. Grandma is ailing still. Grandma said that sex is the glue. Grandma said, and she knew from experience, *never leave your home*. Great literature: the only thing on earth that doesn't scare me. Greener pastures, read every day. Grow my brain and my knowledge. Grow out bangs. Grow up.

Had a dream the night before I bought this new bed that the reason I was short and had stayed short was because I was still sleeping in my childhood bed. Had a little coffee in a small place with a soft chair and started reading her copy of the Javier Marías, enjoying her notes. Had a shower, got dressed, went to buy toilet paper, had tea, sat down at the computer. Had always known that he hoped to kill himself when his body started failing, but I always thought he would choose a different method, not something like jumping from a bridge. Had an intimate conversation with Lemons today. Had sex with Fiona. Hair: don't colour it, don't cut it. Half a lifetime ago we had that conversation. Half my life ago! Halloween to-night. Halloween! Hand your book in and publish it, come what may. Hanif agreed that you must finish what you start as a writer, because otherwise you don't learn anything.

Hanif and his wife were less close, he said, when they weren't having sex. Hanif considers writing in a diary writing! Hanif gave me the sense that such men could love, and that such a love could be strong and devoted, which was what was scaring me. Hanif had a mother who kicked him out; that's life, there is no other mother. Hanif has a wife and a child. Hanif has an inner strength which might be called integrity. Hanif is an intimidating man. Hanif is better onstage than I am, and so is everyone. Hanif met the woman literally of his dreams, the woman he had been writing about his entire life. Hanif once said, *young people never want the gifts of their cultural inheritance.* Hanif said he has no heroes because everyone disappoints you eventually. Hanif said he was publishing two books this year and that he published two last year, which means a lot of travelling. Hanif said he wouldn't be a better writer there; that being a good writer is about staying close to your roots, and that a writer must stay close to their home. Hanif said his books were about longing, and that that was the substance of the universe—longing. Hanif said I had an amazing personality that would serve me well in whatever I chose. Hanif told him not to buy a house on the coast line, that coast lines everywhere will be gone in twenty years. Hanif said it's pretty good if only one out of three years is bad. Hanif said that a man's sexuality is to have a wife and a mistress, both.

Hanif said that discretion, the discreet, is the mode of the warrior. Hanif said that if the woman was the centre of the man's life, that if he truly loved her and was devoted to her, then even if he played around, she could be satisfied. Hanif said that we tend to feel the need to punish ourselves, to stay in our rooms and write. Hanif said, *I think I sense something in you that would be drawn to that*. Hanif said, *well, there's a kind of conservative strain*, and I interrupted, *you think I have a conservative strain?* and he said, *no no, there's a kind of conservative strain that I see other people having, that you don't have*. Hanif said, *you must learn fear—when you meet a guy like this, sure they're attractive, but the thing is to feel afraid and run in the opposite direction*. Hanif said, *you're at a point in your life now where you can make that sort of change*. Hanif said, *you're in control of your life, right?* Hanif said, *you're not going to change when you're forty and have been doing this for twenty years—dating guys with substance abuse problems*. Hanif sat beside me at dinner and the food was wonderful. Hanif says the writer has to get over his guilt and write passionately and with conviction, no shame. Hanif seems to know so much more about the world and writing than I do—so does everyone—and last night at dinner I couldn't talk, I was so choked up with feelings of being unable to speak, and all the men—how they dominated everything, and me being unable to speak because of a suffocating need to be polite.

Hanif talked about the unconscious; how even if it doesn't exist, now it in fact does. Hanif thinks that craft is what writers concern themselves with when they have no subject or passion by birthright. Hanif thought society was the creation of women. Hanif told me that I should watch what Lars does, not what he says, and of course what he did was leave and not call for a week. Hanif told me that this was his first festival and that he generally stays away from other writers—is friends with doctors and mechanics and other such people, because he doesn't want to think that the literary world has any importance. Hanif turned to me with a smile on his face and said of the crowd, *this is not normal.* Hanif wanted to teach his daughter not to look for The One. Hanif was concerned and listened carefully, and it was really nice, and his advice was good, and so was his certainty that I could change. Hanif was telling me the story of two people he knew whose vanity was so great that they *could not even do the single necessary thing, which is to confer the dignity and status of a human being upon their son, by naming him.* Hanif, seeing that I was drinking grape juice, asked for grape juice as well. Hanif's wife turned out to be very beautiful, at least in her passport photo, with a mournful, round face, dark hair, and perfect skin and cupid's-bow lips. Harold Innis, Marshall McLuhan, David Cronenberg, Glenn Gould. Has he made himself into a personality, as he says those artists who become the most talked-about do? Have a balcony to sit and read on. Have integrity in daily life and maintain overall health. Have the story done by Saturday, then do some walking. Have to figure out how much it would cost me to move to California. Haven't figured out how to have this new kind of conversation I'm after, perhaps because I only know what I don't want it to be about—me or the other person's life. Having taken out of the library the book about Schiller. He agreed very solemnly that one has to say yes to everything. He and I both love sleeping in the loft, up near the ceiling. He asked me if part of my insecurity this weekend was from him seeing two women without me, and I said I didn't think so, that I didn't feel threatened by them— even if I did, a bit—and he said, *of all people!* meaning of all women to be threatened by, which one can also interpret badly, like that there *are* women I should be threatened by. He asks me if I want to be his mother, if that would be okay. He has an aggressive quality, a dominating quality, which I find hard to be around, and which often hurts and saddens me. He has an opinion about everything. He has become softer and sadder. He is a former junkie, and he does seem like a man who has lived a hard life and experienced a lot, but Hanif said his reason for never drinking was that he grew up in a tough neighbourhood where everyone drank and was expected to drink, and that he never liked other people telling him what to do. He is always encouraging me to write, and yesterday walking home alone I thought of telling him, *I don't need another superego*. He is awfully nice. He is refreshing and he cheers me up; he makes me happy and I always feel so alive around him. He is so different from me that he can never really get inside my brain in the same way I inhabit my own brain, or in the way that other men have weaseled themselves into my brain. He is such a fine-looking man, so incredibly sexy. He is such a strong, intoxicating man. He is thirty-eight. He is very much blocked and in a boring sort of rut which will carry on for however long, and I have no interest in helping him out of it, or in watching him climb out of it, if he ever does. He isn't really the person I most want to talk to. He just sits there and stares at his computer. He leaned in and gave me a big kiss on the cheek. He lets me have my space, and he cannot pay rent if he lives with me, but he wants not to be poor, and if luck is on his side, he might not be. He makes me look with love on all the people I have ever loved, and honour them all. He moved to New York, and the city would have taken advantage of him if he didn't toughen up, so he did, he says, and now he feels better in the world. He moved to Paris for seven years and now he is back here, adjusting. He must have no idea how differently this relationship is sitting in me, or how differently it's directing me, but probably I have no notion of how differently it's resting in him. He must know that he is making me suffer, not to have called for two days, when it used to be that we talked all the time; I guess his love for me flared up, then died away. He needs to feel superior over a woman in every way, for he is a thirty-three-year-old man who has accomplished nothing. He said he didn't think women were that way, wanting to sleep with a man after already deciding they don't like him. He said he has never dated a woman younger than him. He said he heard me stop crying as soon as he left the house, so he knew in the future not to believe my tears. He said he understood my throwing away his phone number. He said it would be interesting if I got pregnant in the middle of writing this book, and I walked away from that conversation at Le Poisson Rouge feeling he was right. He said maybe the Cold War phase of our relationship could come to an end. He said that his unresolved situation with me is part of what caused the break-up with his girlfriend, and last night at the bar he said I ought to go to Mexico for a week, and in bed he kept proposing these fantasies where he would come over once a day and fuck me and then leave, or we'd have tea together every afternoon and a fuck and he'd leave; he also believes I must live alone. He said to me, *I could really make you my slut*. He said, correcting me, that he didn't want to be an architect, but rather that his father kicked him out of the house, so he picked architecture. He says he needs to do one or two big architectural projects here because he has all these connections; he can't very well leave here with nothing and start over again from zero. He says I can build myself a little house on his land and go there to write. He sits in front of the TV when sports are on and cheers quietly to himself so he will not disturb me. He talked differently with me and my friends than he does with other people. He told me that after seeing my thigh that day, when I was reading in one of the common rooms downstairs and wearing my green skirt, he couldn't work for an hour or think about anything else—so that was pretty good. He told me that one day he would want to have sex with me and another woman. He told me this morning that he didn't think it was morally justifiable to watch pornography, so he doesn't, and he gave me his reasons, one of which was that it increases the misogyny in society. He took the blindfold off and asked me if I wanted to stop or continue. He was saying my name over and over as I was sucking his cock, and when he came, he came silently, without a sound, just a contraction, his body straining, his hands clutching my head tighter, holding me down on him, his whole hips coming forward and pressing his dick in my mouth, holding me there so I felt like I was underwater while he came in my mouth. He was very understanding, and in gratitude I wrote him a very emotional and grateful letter, emphasizing my point about us needing to be separate people. He was wonderful and I didn't treat him right, I could only see him sexually, I never took him seriously. He won't return my calls or talk to me, and I feel so mad, it feels horrible not to be loved by him. He's a traitor. Hell, get him to edit it. Her criticisms of me go deep, but they are very accurate—I used to bristle at them, but now I see them as having truth. Her desire to be reclusive speaks well of her. Her dirty hands. Her hair curled slightly. Her husband of eight years. Her mother died when she was young. Her sexual organs are inside her, so her life should remain inside her; she should let her ideas grow slowly, secretly and privately inside. Her stories are good in a way, they're very animal and very embodied. High on mushrooms in the park yesterday, Lemons asked me to tell him the story of my last relationship. His body was not the body for me, but rather every other man's was. His eyes were pale blue and I followed him around. His face continued to blush, then he got what seemed to be tears in his eyes and said, *oh good, because you should have my baby*. His hand on my back at the bar—I will never forget how held and protected I felt, how strong his hand was, or how real it felt against my back. His ideal is not to have to think about the relationship, he said, but to have some woman cook for him, and he can do his own thing, and they can sit together and read the newspaper at night. His life is so dug into New York with his theatre company, and mine is in Toronto; these practical things matter as one gets older. His mother telling him to settle down and stop being so transient, that a rolling stone gathers no moss. His name is not a romantic name; it's a name that cuts. His name sounds like a knife, flashing. His profile is so nice when he sleeps. His room is a little cold and his two thin blankets are never enough. Holding it up like a dirty cloth, Rosa said, *what is this thing?* Honesty gets ugly here. How am I going to pay rent next month? How awful that she could see that. How bad could it possibly get if I rested for a time? How can I possibly write when I'm obsessed with my relationships? How can I tell a story about what happens to other people if I cannot even remember stories from my own life, or how certain changes occurred? How can you guess what's in another person's head? How can you live if to some extent you do not see life as a game, with the feeling that there is winning and losing, and strategies for winning, and that there are rules by which one plays the game, which other people are also playing? How can you live in this way when you never would write in this way? How can you love someone you've known for only two weeks? How deeply ashamed I am for even thinking it. How did I come to have all these animals sleeping with me in my bed? How disappointed I am to have wasted that magical and rich feeling, instead becoming angrier as the day went on, with Rosa wanting to see me when I don't have the time, and the cell phone battery salesman—what a crook—and a million other things! How do you express both things in literature: that there is a person, and that the person is dressed up as the character? How do you show both without showing that you are showing both? How does a person accept their flawed humanity and forgive themselves for causing pain, and for not rising to the occasion constantly? How does he pick the most irritating, shallow, superficial, terrible wives? How does someone dismantle themselves? How does someone shift their axis? How exhausting! How fast the days are going! How Goethe put all of himself into *The Sorrows of Young Werther*. How hard is it to reply? How infantile! How is one not self-loathing? How is this a betrayal? How it is a tragedy that you only get to be yourself in this life. How little you think of how sincerely you are judged by others for real, lasting and serious flaws in your character, instead fearing judgment in this neurotic way, as if one little email you send could incur their severest condemnation; as if you are not really seen. How long I wanted to be rid of myself—but couldn't be. How many people did I have sex with this year? How many people did I kiss? How much I enjoy pleasure. How much pleasure there is in just sitting around, writing, eating and reading. How nice it is to contemplate new things for a change, and how good it would be to do that every day, just as last night we contemplated the stars, another day it could be a tree; how many experiences are available to us in the nearest vicinity that we do not grasp hold of, let alone all those experiences at a further distance. How nice it is to have all these lovers, whatever happens with them. How nice it would be if one could actually rely on them. How random life is! How strange if all this was just to end in me finally returning to Pavel. How strange, as someone would say of a dream. How stupid to go from such happiness one day, to feeling such revulsion for oneself the next, from one day feeling joy, to there being no possibility of it at all the next. How tiresome it is getting older.

I act like a woman. I adore him. I almost collapsed writing that story. I almost think it's better than the book. I always feel like if I don't look at my life closely enough, I'm abandoning some important task, but maybe that's not true. I always felt that writing was sort of a waste of time and I shouldn't do it, then I overcame that this year, but I still have that feeling about reading, which is what I must overcome this year. I always felt unhappy when I didn't have a boyfriend, even when I was two. I always forget how long life is. I always forget this like an idiot. I always had a desire to be other than I was—to be another person, just for a second, an hour, a day. I always think I don't write much, but I actually probably write quite a lot. I always think I will never hear from him again, and I'm always fine with this—that it's over. I always thought a relationship had to go as high up as it possibly could—marriage—then destroy itself. I always want things to be done when I say they are, but things have to work their way entirely through your system, like food in digestion. I am a spineless person. I am absolutely not a shark in any way. I am all alone in my hotel room, longing for a person. I am cancelling appointments with people. I am checking email once a day and reading in the mornings. I am completely exhausted with myself and it is not yet eight in the morning. I am doing my work. I am doing what I need to be doing. I am drinking tea out of bone china and eating cherries on a warm, sunny day. I am eating thick white bread with butter, and beside my plate is a pot of the marmalade that Giovanna's neighbour made, and I am drinking water with bubbles, and coffee from a wide, white cup. I am excited about lying around in bed with him, reading quietly to ourselves. I am finished with my book, but my book is not finished with me. I am foul-minded today. I am getting that specific pain in my hands that comes when I feel he is ignoring or neglecting me. I am getting tired but I will press on. I am getting tired of this life, I suppose, and I was impatient all night, and impatient while having a cigarette with Pavel downstairs. I am getting tired of writing this book. I am getting to the point where I feel like I've mapped the land. I am glad he is coming because I am growing sick of being in my head. I am glad he is out of town right now. I am glad I'm not going to be around all those cookies and candies anymore. I am going inside myself and I don't want to have coffee with anyone anymore! I am going to buy the sandals that I'll wear all summer. I am going to check my email, then work hard the rest of the day. I am going to have an apartment on the second floor or third floor, and there will be a balcony there, and space, and people can come over if they want to. I am going to Istanbul on Saturday. I am going to miss this creamy, high-ceilinged room. I am going to think about thoughts. I am happy because there is nothing I want. I am happy I am not with someone who minces and pleads, but who states things strongly and articulately. I am happy with my solitude, punctuated by close friends. *I am having the best sex of my life*, she told us, and as we left, she walked off with her husband, hand in hand, saying, *we're going down to the root cellar now*. I am in a rage and a jealous rage right now. I am in a really bad mood, really self-pitying. I am in Istanbul. I am in New York. I am in Paris with nothing to do but be here for two more weeks. I am in the new hotel, it's nearly six in the morning, another night when I could not sleep. I am just a freelance reporter. I am just a reporter without even a place to put the story I most want to write. I am just sitting here moping and feeling terrible. I am lazy and do not like to work. I am less full of doubt than usual. I am looking forward to just rolling around with him on the carpet and in the grass and in my bed. I am looking forward to writing and the beauty and rhythm of the sentences I will write, to outlining a world, and making it real, and taking the conventions for granted, and seeing what is the best thing I can make. I am nauseous a lot of the time, I don't know why, a little bug? I am not ambitious to be published in *The New Yorker*. I am not ambitious to have a grand love, I just want to have a nice one. I am not ambitious to live in New York and know all the fancy people, it's enough for me to know only a few. I am not going to break it off for I do feel sexually faithful to him, and have felt that way since the beginning; as though when he takes his dick out of me, he leaves a lock in its place. I am not Leonard Cohen. I am not sure that I like this realization. I am not sure. I am on my way to London and am sitting on the plane. I am on my way to Montreal on the train. I am perfectly content to let others speak, even if I get jealous while they are speaking, that they have allotted themselves the time. I am reading about artists' studios. I am reading the Ripley novels now. I am really beginning to feel what freedom might mean and how far it might stretch. I am sad. I am scared. I am sick of this going-nowhereness, these games. I am sick of this wondering, this guessing, this uncertainty and instability. I am sincere with him, I guess. I am single now. I am sitting at my little table. I am sitting here in a light blue dress, the dress I bought yesterday at Kensington Market. I am sitting in bed and feeling nothing. I am sitting outside in the blue hammock. I am so happy I will be seeing Lars in two days! I am so happy I'm going to be seeing him in New York. I am so happy the book is done. I am so happy today. I am so sick of myself and all my thoughts, circles, fears, and worries. I am so tired I want to die. I am spending too much money. I am starting to feel like life is not for having experiences, so that therefore one can make deductions about life and one's personality, and then make up rules for the future by which one can live and therefore attain happiness and perfection. I am starting to feel sorry for Pavel for having a girlfriend like me. I am still a little drunk. I am still in the hotel room, sitting on the bed. I am still sick, and I'm upset about him not communicating with me since my texts. I am still young, twenty-eight. I am such a fool. I am taking over from the last actress. *I am taking the year off,* Tom said, his legs dangling in the pool. I am thinking about giving up my crushes. I am thinking again about Lars. I am thinking about the man from last night who played the piano. I am thirty-one, after all. I am thirty-two. I am through with them all! I am through with talking, but I still want the company of other people. I am tired as hell right now. I am tired of always pushing myself, pushing myself. I am tired of feeling so tired all the time, so depressed and wanting to cry. I am too overwhelmed right now, so on the tail end of these changes and feeling scattered. I am too tired to go out into the world. I am too ugly to be in a video on YouTube. I am trying to learn from the Helen DeWitt book, but what is there to learn except that it works? I am wearing his tank top as I sit on his bed. I am wearing my hair pulled off my face. I am writing this letter to Pavel because it will be too hard to say it. I apologized to him, and now there is just the rest of my life. I arrived before noon, but my room wasn't ready, so I went for a walk and went through the gates of the castle in Vincennes; there is a moat around it filled with grass. I asked Claire if she felt different now that she had all this success, which seemed like the most obvious question in the world, but she really paused and was like, *hmm, that's a really good question*, then she explained that so much had changed, but she wasn't sure what to attribute to what—what to her new film, what to her new boyfriend, what to her new apartment. I asked her if she was making the stars out of silver paper, and she said, *no, sandpaper*. I asked her what she is most good at in the world, and she said it was making—writing, directing, she wasn't sure what to call it—and I asked what her technique was, and she said, *I do it every day*. I asked her whether deadlines are important and she said, *yes, because they provide a container*. I asked him if he cheated on me because our sex was bad or unsatisfying, and he said no, not at all. I asked him what his best quality as a boyfriend was and what was his worst, and he said, *you first*, so I said that the worst was my changeability and the best was how loving I am, and he acted shocked that I considered myself loving. I bought a polka-dot scarf at A.P.C. I bought a red Yves Saint Laurent lipstick. I bought some salty salmon, a bagel, a salad of cucumbers, mozzarella balls and tomato, some popcorn, a chocolate bar with white mint filling—it was those words, *white mint*, which made me want to buy it—and I ate it with the Brie I had back at my hotel. I broke a mirror trying to see if my shoes matched my outfit, and finally went out in the heels, not the boots, because I knew the proportions with the boots would be off. I broke up with him over the weekend. I called him an *erotic burr*, an awful thing to say. I came back to bed and prayed for a while—prayed that God would show me the direction to take with my next book. I came in this morning and noticed that the pin was gone from the table, but I didn't know what to attribute it to, then I forgot about it, but not before remembering that he wasn't a real architect, he had just studied architecture, and he had never fixed my table, despite claiming that he would. I came to my computer and started working on my book, understanding it more and more. I can continue going in this direction. I can do it. I can do this, too. I can do whatever I want. I can ease off the pressure. I can have a bigger imagination than to think, *New York or L.A.?* I can hold a much more complex picture in my head. I can look at my bookshelves. I can look over that high wall. I can only hide my pain and sadness so much. I can starve or asphyxiate the part of my brain that thinks about men. I can't help but think that he doesn't really love me, that his love has cooled, and that if he was really excited about me, he would find a pay phone and call. I can't let this year be like the last. I can't remember the last time I ever felt so worn out, so having nothing left to give, so at the end and half-dead. I can't remember the last time I felt so bad. I can't sleep in the same bed as him. I capitulate, I take polls, I do what other people think I should do. I catalogued it in my head this way: *friends, lovers, loneliness, art.* I cried when I was talking to Pavel later in the evening about his pure heart, explaining why it made sense to me that she had trusted him not to cheat. I decided to be indifferent towards my romantic future and to not try and escape my fate, which is what I have always done, having always been afraid of my fate, which is a reflection of my character, certain it is a bad one—bad character, bad fate. I decided when I got home that I would not fight with him anymore, though of course that decision is pointless, it happens without either of us anticipating it and it comes out of real tensions. I denigrate my relationship in the face of other relationships I see, imagining mine is at the bottom of the heap. I deserve to work, to whittle away everything known as a life. I did not remember that I asked to see his penis, which apparently really upset him. I didn't realize how awful and depressed he felt. I didn't say good-bye to him because I kind of couldn't bear to. I don't completely understand when Ellis says, *the novel is a fundamentally ironic form, hence its power of self-regeneration.* I don't even know what that means. I don't feel I'm all that perceptive, mainly because I live in a cloud of my own making. I don't have as much faith in Lemons as a good editor since he turned down my book. I don't have to be the kind of woman he predicts I will be. I don't have to tell the world my version of events. *I don't know every artist,* I replied mildly. *I don't know how you do it,* the young man across from me said, seeing me typing so fast, not looking at the keys. I don't know if I want to write fiction next, or write this third book, or do projects that have no result, or move out of the city, or move out of the city for just half the year, or stay with him for two weeks in the fall. I don't know if this is what some women call the feeling of wanting to have a baby—all I know is that all I can think about is sex, and I have an insatiable hunger that he cannot satisfy, and which I know could not be satisfied by any kind of man or any kind of sex. I don't know what will be the end of this. I don't know what's going to happen next. I don't know why Lemons insists on predicting things for me. I don't know; maybe she's good to her grandmother. I don't mean this as a bad thing, but I just realized that nothing happens in a life. I don't need to ask him why he wants to be with me, because it's obvious to me on some very basic level that I could never put into words, for I assume it's a mirror for the thing inside me that makes a beeline for him. I don't remember how we started kissing, I mean, I remember that he leaned over and kissed me, and that we had been lying there close together and touching for maybe half an hour; perhaps it was just that I finally put the glass on the floor, then turned around and looked at him. I don't think there's anything left to think about—that is, I don't think there are any more epiphanies left to have. I don't want a life in Paris. I don't want a party. I don't want just any man, I want Lars, even if there is something dangerous about being with him. I don't want to be a mother to a man. I don't want to be dead in four years. I don't want to go to any more parties. I don't want to go to L.A. I don't want to go to New York, but I have to for the book. I don't want to talk to my friends about him, and I feel like I don't want anyone's opinion or thoughts on my life ever again. I explained to Ellis that Lemons had met this woman, and that she seemed to me a shallow, jealous, unpleasant, bossy kind of girl, but that if he was lucky, and Ellis and I laughed about this, he, too, would find a superficial, jealous, petty-minded woman and believe her to be the most perfect thing in the world. I feel a little better. I feel excited! I feel flushed. I feel he is my enemy for saying this, and that Lemons can't possibly take me seriously if he is suggesting that I publish the book now. I feel like crying. I feel so much fear and reticence and apology and stress. I feel so much with Lars, but there's an element of fantasy at the root of it all—we have never really been together, we exist out of reach from each other, because that is how we serve each other best. I fell short of asking who was better in bed, Laurel or me. I felt really sick in the morning and went to the pharmacy—I so love the pharmacies in Spain!—and the pharmacist stirred some powdered Tylenol or cold mix into a glass of water, and put it on the counter for me as it fizzed up. I felt so pretty in those A.P.C. clothes. I felt so pretty trying on those clothes in A.P.C.! I felt, the other night, so happy with my book. I finally said he looked like Rambo, and he said, *Arthur Rimbaud?* I find it interesting that some people are not going to the American ambassador's house tomorrow night for cocktails as a protest against the foreign policies of the United States. I find it tiresome. I finished a chapter of *The Sheltering Sky*, sitting on the porch, and came in to find that it was 8:21, time to go down for dinner, which Giovanna's cook had prepared. I got down on my knees behind the tree and sucked his cock for a while. I got drunk and flirted a lot. I got hysterical and threw a drink on him because I thought it was the thing to do. I got my favourite toothpaste, Elgydium. I got my period last night when the moon was full. I had him jerk off for me and he licked his hand before doing it. I hate him these days! I hate how he always asks me to tell him about my day, which always feels like he is trying to take my experiences away from me. I hate that I can't remember anyone's name. I hate the feeling that someone in the world hates me. I hated my brain tonight. I hated talking with Lemons last night, his not understanding what relationships are for; saying he thought that people were afraid to be alone. I have a bad stomach ache right now. I have a blister on my foot. I have a headache now from crying. I have a horrible jealous streak in me, not about money but about boyfriends—upset that Agnes has had better boyfriends than me, more successful, handsome, desirable and kind. I have a knife in my heart and I want them all to die. I have a lump in my throat or perhaps a swelling that's making it hard to breathe. I have a tendency, when things are a little bad, to think they are the worst they could possibly be. I have a way of reducing the humanity of the man I am with to a manageable size, and it is something I mustn't do—it is what I saw my mother do. I have been sick all winter with so many different colds. I have been tired these days, but that's probably just winter. I have cleaned my apartment except for the kitchen and the bathroom floors. I have failed as a human. I have more respect for those who want to change the world and social conditions than those who want to change themselves and their relationships. I have my event in two and a half hours. I have never been so screwed for money, and I am angry at Lemons for not returning my emails. I have never known what a relationship is for. I have never worn such dark lipstick before. I have no money. I have no one. I have spent the whole night in my hotel room, eating chocolate cereal. I have started playing Tetris, which feels halfway between writing and drinking. I have sunk to the bottom of my ambition, career-wise. I have to learn to value the grey pallor of existence. I have to move my body. I have to read Tom McCarthy's book. I have to rest. I have to think about it when I'm more awake, and it's no longer five o'clock in the morning. I have to work faster, or write more books, or books that will sell more. I have to write that thing for the *Financial Times*. I heard the door to the third floor swing open. I hit him and he poured his beer on me. I hope my last email didn't scare him off! I hoped he'd look at me again, since I was wearing the new bra. I hung out with Claire and we went to the Tate Modern, and we talked as we walked amidst the art, not really seeing the art. I increasingly cannot imagine a life with children; I would rather be alone, looking out over the waves from a beach house in some coastal town. I keep life pretty simple, actually. I keep thinking about Lars and how he said, *the next time you like a guy, don't leave the city*. I kissed everyone hello. I kissed him and saw his smile in the night. I knew a big love would come about in the spring of my thirty-second year. I knew when I was young that all that mattered for art was conviction. I know this cannot be interesting to read. I know this. I know what I am. I know what they're saying. I laughed and couldn't stop laughing. I laughed into my hand. I lay down in my bed, checking my phone for text messages. I lay very still. I like Claire more since her outburst. *I like dark and dusty corners*, I said, and Pavel said, *I do too*, and we relaxed. I like him and don't in about equal measure, and love him and hate him in about equal amounts. I like him on one level, but what a bore and so completely devoid of self-knowledge on the other. I like how he smells, I love how it feels to hold him, I like how intelligent he is, I like his family, I love how he treats his friends, I like how good-looking he is, I like his balanced view of the world and his moral nature, even if he can be an asshole sometimes. I like how he wrapped my present in tracing paper and silver duct tape. I like my face. I like my life and what I have created for myself. I like reading Gogol. I like reading Oscar Wilde. I like reading reviews in the *NYRB* of collections of essays put out by art critics. I like seeing the old women swimming; it makes being old seem not so bad. I like that I don't have to take care of him, and I like how excited, desirous and adoring I feel, when I'm not feeling annoyed and hateful. I like that Pavel wants me, and that he's so strange, strange in that extreme no-culture way—that is, he doesn't belong to any tribe you can pinpoint, and is a complete non-conformist in the authentic way, in the way that makes everyone want to beat him up. I like the way the pastries are taken out of their dishes, put onto paper plates, then wrapped in flower-covered wrapping paper, the sides tucked in and under. I like thinking, and I love tools for thinking. I like this apartment so much, it's my obvious home. I like this feeling of getting just a little bit fat. I like to take art slow, as slow as it needs. I like what I was writing last winter. I liked eating at Caffe Brasiliano; I mean to say that it matched my mood to talk about who in the city we hated and trivial stuff like that. I liked seeing him smoke that last puff of a ciga-rette, throwing it out before the doors opened and we walked into the airport together. I liked walking through the back alleys the other day as I was heading to Vig's house, think-ing of him waiting for me in the dead of night. I lit the candelabra; there were five candles on it. I loathe my sexual attraction to men. I long for him and love him and pine for him, even when we're in the same room together. I looked at her on the internet, and she's not what I thought she'd look like, in fact she kind of looks like me, and I wonder whether they have sex in the same way we did. I love embroilments.

I love him so! I love him very much. I love him, I do. I love his soft skin, and I want to hold him in my arms, and I love his voice, and how much I want to just crack him open and climb inside him. I love his voice, yelling in the other room. I love how he says *huh?* so quietly and gently, his eyes all innocent and boy-like. I love how he uses that word for it, *cock*, and I came, though mildly, just from fucking him last night. I love how I don't know his face yet. I love that phrase of the art critic, *I write poetry for my assistants*. I love the entire universe and everything in it. I love the food he cooks for me, and I wake up happy every morning after a night of dreaming about him. I love to wake and see Vig's face. I loved that woman with the cross-eyes, though I am never perfectly sure which eye to look into. I loved the other day when he showed me how the newspaper was new, folding over the sports and arts sections, I just watched him and how he is a marvel. I made a coffee and now I'm drinking it. I mean, seeing him standing there in the shelter of the subway, I wondered what it would be like to be with a man like that—with a red leather briefcase and an overcoat on. I must be ovulating. I mustn't rush it, but it is, as he said, like a weather pattern coming over the horizon; you can no more stop love than you can stop the weather pattern from moving. I need a new bra. I need money. I need to be less modest, and to see the worth of the kind of thinking that comes naturally to me. I need to get over my guilt in order to write narrative. I never felt more deliciously alone—more away from people, or from culture—than when I was having sex with Pavel. I never know, when I'm sitting down to write, where people go or what they do. I never meet any new people. I never meet any of the interesting people there are to meet. I never met Kafka, yet I feel like I have. I never met Thomas Bernhard. I never regret anything that happened more than a few days ago. I never used to cry at all. I once believed that making art was going to bring me happiness and success and be this pretty thing. I once said to someone, *I know who I'm in a relationship with because that's the person I'm thinking of breaking up with.* I only realized it today. I only think about art. I only think about what I want and need. I only try to please a little bit. I prefer my life when I'm quiet and writing, not smoking and travelling. I protested that it's not so easy to stop taking someone into consideration when you have been concerned about them for five whole years, but as I said this, I opened the door to the deli and saw the long salad bar halfway down the store, and all the ingredients in it, and its silver roof, and it felt possible to never think of him again. I pulled my bangs back because of a conversation with Rosa. I put down the new blue-and-cream tablecloth, and placed upon it the very mediocre results of a lamb recipe, so now I'm going to throw that cookbook out. I put his shirts to my face and inhale them when he's away, no matter how bad a time we are having. I put on eye make-up. I put the teeth in my pocket. I read some of *The Fall of Public Man*. I read the Henry Miller essay about painting. I realize more and more these days that people finish things and live in a world of time, rather than not finishing or taking forever for the sake of the eternal. I realize that I cannot expect to be very advanced in life when only nine months ago I was in Europe performing with a band, which was ridiculous and a disaster. I realize that I'm a very bad observer, and that on some level I don't really notice anything, or perhaps I don't trust what I notice, or don't put it into words. I realized how rarely my mother praised me, so how meaningful it is each time, and how much of a surprise, always, when I get an indication that she likes me. I realized I did it to get a thrill, the way I would look forward to thrills when I was a child, and publishing has become one such thrill, and Twitter, too, but it's good to cut out thrill-seeking because I think it makes me happier to have a base of calm, so I should ask myself when something seems like a good idea, *is this thrill-seeking or adrenalin-seeking behaviour?* I realized I had become impractical in my thinking about money, losing sight of its value and how long it takes me to make any. I realized that that's what I've been doing—looking for a mother in everyone. I really am a man in that way. I really am an indoors person, I guess I always have been. I really am too tired to write. I really do love him so much. I really do love him! I really do want to be on the beach on January 1st of this year, just as I wanted that last year, and to see the sun rise—it's what I want more than anything, if the sun even rises there, I don't know. I really don't want to find out I'm pregnant this month. I really have no love left for him, practically. I said I loved him, too. I said that I often asked older people what this age was, and all of them said, *it's the beginning of your life*. I said to him that it was okay for an artist not to be up on what's absolutely current, but if an artist loses their heart, they're useless. I said to Rosa that it makes me very happy to do things for my roommate, and I told her of how I had given him the bigger room, and she said, *wow, maybe you really* are *ready for a real relationship*. I said, *I can't publish it in English though*, which made Amandine livid, and she said, *you must publish it in English!* and I said, *I don't know*. I said, *I sure don't have any other friends like you*, and Lemons said, *I sure don't have any other friends like you*. I said, *this is romantic, having dinner here with you*, and Claire agreed that it was. I sat down and he sat behind me, and we made out as the waves from the sea rolled up and wet us, and he fingered me, and my jeans were covered in salt, and I looked out at the sea, and the night was above us, and so were the stars, and I was conscious of how this was the most romantic scene I had ever been in, but I knew I was too conscious of this fact for it to actually be so. I sat next to Ellis, and the old writer's wife sat on the other side, and for the most part engaged him in conversation, so that although I talked to him, I did not talk to him as much as I would have liked, and at the end of the night he left to work on an article which he was on deadline for, which I could understand, but I felt sad. I sat on the counter and watched Pavel make pasta. I sat on the train and felt saddened and sickened. I say things and he is just quiet. I see men with qualities I admire and wish to possess, and I make them my lovers, rather than trying to develop those qualities in myself. I sent Pavel to the door, then at the last minute pulled him back. I should go to bed soon. I should go to sleep. I should live according to my feelings and see what comes—that is, my independent feelings, not feelings which are attempts to mirror other people's feelings. I should not be so flattered if a man gets an erection around me. I should not neglect the plant. I should not write Ellis off as a golden boy. I should remember that literature is the dark arts, and is probably not going to save my life or wind me up in some pretty, happy, conventional place. I should try to trust my past selves to have made the right decisions, and not think my past selves were so stupid that I must always be second-guessing the decisions they made. I shouldn't be so hard on myself; so for ten minutes I was messing around with Vig and wasn't enjoying myself—who cares? I shouldn't want a man who only six months ago was a drug addict—it's not long enough clean. I slept all day. I slept and slept. I slept at Amandine's place that night, and the next day I went with her and the British guy to the apartment she had lived in for ten years, her first apartment in Paris, and we packed up the last of her stuff, and I walked up and down the five narrow twisting flights of stairs with her garbage, and left it out by the curb where it was picked over by the people who passed in the street, then I went into an antique shop and broke a teacup which was part of a set of six teacups and saucers from the eighteenth century, but the woman was very nice about it, and though I kept saying, *ah, mon Dieu*, she said, *eet is my problem for putting ze teacup zair!* I slept in my childhood bed until I was twenty-nine. I smile as I write this. I so much enjoy just thinking. I spent all fucking day making a roast and two apple pies, and the roast didn't turn out, and neither did the pies. I spent all my money on a coat this winter and it wasn't even cold enough to wear it for one week. I spent it all in one night—my dignity, everything. I spent most of the day writing and talking to people on the phone, sitting on the toilet and talking to Lemons, letting him tell me all the gossip. I spoke about how Laurel had been an academic, and how she and her boyfriend would fuck two times a day, and how when I asked her how she got any work done during the years that she was with him, she said she didn't; she didn't get anything done. I started neglecting the plant when Lars didn't respect it. I sublet my apartment for July, showing it to one person and corresponding with another. I suddenly had a feeling tonight that as much as I think I want to move to L.A. or run in these big circles, I am happiest in my anonymity and in my head, without having to make compromises, and without having to deal with anything too scary, just me alone in my fantasy world. I suggested that it wasn't the contemporary style. I suppose as a mathematician attends to math, a writer has to attend to the human drama. I suppose that's the part I don't understand: how to make art out of this new place. I think I'm sad. I think my dreamy father, a pleasure-seeker, didn't prepare me for the harshness and the difficulty of life. I thought about saying that I liked her movies, but didn't say it, figuring she got that all the time and not wanting to be a bother, or for her to turn on whatever she typically turns on when people say that to her. I thought that humans, on the whole, were not so great, not as great as they're made out to be. I told Claire about how he had drawn, with his cock, a circle on my belly before entering me, and she was kind of moved by it in the way that I had been; she totally got it. I told Claire that I didn't have a memory, and she said, *thus the recordings*, which was so smart and intimate and intuitively right and understanding. I told Claire that the problem with both having a relationship and being devoted to making art was that thing in the Bible, that man cannot serve two masters, but she said she thought that it was not a conflict because we would be serving, in both cases, the same master: the heart. I told her about how things had been with Pavel, and how he seemed like a baby in diapers by the end. I told her about when he asked me to be his girlfriend, how I said I couldn't because the word was too big, but also not big enough. I told her that I couldn't drink another glass of champagne, and she said, *do you think you drink too much?* I told her that I couldn't love a man who couldn't spell, it was impossible. I told him his gait was similar to Belmondo's. I told him his luck was about to change. I told him on the couch that I wanted us to be real friends, and that I thought we could be. I told him that being with him felt like coming home. I told him that he was feeling sorry for himself, and that it was bullshit, that we could have had something. I told him that I had more sexual jealousy with him than with any other guy I'd been with, and he said it was a time of transition for him, then he went down on me, and he was doing it in such a meditative and connected way, which hadn't been the case for so long. I told him that I still hadn't written the book I most wanted to write, which talks about the beauty of the world, and what is so great about being alive. I told Lemons about the feeling I had that something big would happen at the end of the year—I didn't know what it would be, but I knew it as far back as last December, and that I'd never had a presentiment like it before, and that I had been kind of nervous all year, waiting to see what would happen. I told my brother that I couldn't very well spend all of my time burying my head in Pavel's neck, staring at him and carrying him with me everywhere, and telling him a hundred times a day how much I loved him, and he said that's why people have a baby. I told Pavel the truth, that I had forgotten my phone at home and I hadn't seen it in twelve hours, but that upon seeing it, I called him right back. I told the man on the train that if you don't look at the keys you might find that your hands have already memorized the keyboard. I told them about how I wanted be lying on a beach in L.A. in October, ordering books off the internet, and Ellis's girlfriend said, *the only thing that would make it better is if the beach had WiFi.* I took a long walk with Pavel and then went for a swim. I tried on the ruby and gold ring in the antique store, and I found those two shiny aquamarine tiles I bought, and it was all so exhilarating, and I saw how being with a friend in a new city, you were still in relation to the friend, but being alone in a new city, you were entirely in relation to the city itself. I tried saying to myself, *you are in Paris, you are in Paris, you are in Paris,* but the more I said it, the less convinced I felt. I tried to persuade her that she was a real artist, but Claire said she already knew. I visualized blood and her lying there with her head flung back. I want him to push his dick into me for the first time, hard. I want him to push my head back as he fucks me. I want sandals and some new clothes. I want simply to write my next book. I want the book to be amazing. I want to be able to afford to get haircuts, and to wear make-up and nice clothes. I want to be healthy, but then right away after thinking that, I had a cigarette and some wine. I want to be words in a book, and not even that so much. I want to die when he does that. I want to feel his body as he comes, and feel his breath in my ear. I want to get him *Soliloquy.* I want to live my simple life without any interruptions or inconveniences. I want to tear him apart with my teeth and feel his blood all over my mouth. I was about to crash in agony at it having been so long since we made love, largely the fault of the rash. I was all sore—my ears and neck, where he had bit me, pushed me; then today he ran me a pink bubble bath, brought me tea, goat's milk cheese, raspberries, made a roast, and went to AA while I lay there sleeping. I was always watching myself to see what kind of effect I was creating, to create the effect I most wanted to create. I was amazed how much he liked his cock being touched by me when I wasn't even thinking about it, just doing it idly. I was beginning to feel that this part of the year was cursed. I was cutting his hair, pulling it up between my fingers and cutting the hair above my fingers— it was late in the party, I was so drunk, I don't remember who else was there. I was feeling cold and sick, and my shirt wasn't looking right, not with the bra or without it. I was feeling insecure half the day. I was feeling terrible and like I shouldn't have come. I was in a dark and bitter mood. I was lying on the floor and I called him over and he got down on the floor with me and I was stroking his arm. I was not put on this earth to make a man feel good about himself. I was not put on this earth to perform. I was pushing his face away from mine. I was really curious to meet her brother, named after the family dog. I was telling Rosa about him, and she asked me how old he was, and I said forty-four, and she asked if he had kids or if he'd been married, and I said no, and she shook her head and said there was something wrong with a man of forty-four who'd never been married and didn't have kids. I was thinking about how life is long so that lots of growth can happen slowly, while I want it all at once. I was thinking last night, *why does life pair me with such unadvanced men?* but then I thought, *maybe these men* are *advanced.* I was thinking, before Rosa told me what Jung thought God was, that she would say that God was like the eraser on the end of a pencil. I was trying to find a novel, a book, to take with me on the train, feeling as heartsick as I'm feeling, and feeling the coldness of the world, and this harshness and aloneness, and I ended up with a Kurt Vonnegut. I was very nervous as I was getting ready, and I hated myself for changing my clothes and putting on nail polish, as if I were going on a date. I was watching those Bob Dylan press conferences from the sixties and I was thinking, *this is who Goethe would have been if he had been living in the sixties, of course he would have been a folk singer.* I watched through the window as Vig left the garden and went into the street and started writing on his BlackBerry. I welled up with tears. I went back to my room where my clothes were. I went back to sobbing and shouting as he got dressed in the other room. I went for a long walk to get over my bad feelings. I went into some second-hand stores, and in one I felt the man wanted me to leave because I was not dressed cool enough. I went into the bath, then I called out for him to come and see my bruises. I went to return my eye cream to Kiehl's, because I felt I had spent too much money on it, but once there I got an even more expensive one, then I went to the Strand to look at the book that Lemons told me to buy. I went to the Tate Britain and looked at the Turners, which I didn't like at first, but then I found that when I went to the other areas of the museum, I missed the Turners. I went up to the village today and did my email in the small library beside a pimply girl who was gracious but could not help me transfer the file onto my USB, nor could the librarian help me, nor could the man. I will always choose a life with people. I will always have my restlessness. I will finish my book. I will finish those three stories. I will get a new bed. I will get my toe fixed. I will handle a scandal coolly. I will have my last smoke with Pavel tomorrow. I will have to be resourceful and live as cheaply as possible. I will have to write something that sells. I will make it right. I will never cheat on anyone again. I will never forget Lemons saying that at any moment he could have disposed of her like a used Kleenex. I will never know what matters the way that other brains know what matters. I will return to my book, but not with the little duster that one takes in hand when approaching ancient Egyptian tablets, but with a chainsaw and no fear. I will run out of money if I do not finish the book, but otherwise what is the rush? I will try not to think the worst of him. I will wash the sweater with the other stuff. I will write him a letter on paper, expressing my feelings so he knows them. I will write what is necessary to write. I wish he could love me, for he is the man I could see it all happening with. I wish he had more of a sex drive for me, or that we had more sexual chemistry, or that I didn't feel so rejected all the time. I wish he was more intimate and affectionate and less

angry. I wish I could find a way to shut off my brain in regards to Lars, but he has a way that is very puzzling, on the
one hand saying things like, *come with me to Mexico for a
week*, and that his relationship partly ended because he was
thinking of me, and on the other, saying within five minutes
of seeing me that he is still a bit in love with his ex-girlfriend.
I wish I could think about other things—God, spirituality—
but I am suffering by Lars, so I am thinking about Lars. I
wish I could wake up alone in oatmeal. I wish I could write
about everything in a less completely narrow way. I wish I
had never kissed him. I wish I was not awake right now in
the middle of the night. I wish my head didn't feel so full of
junk. I woke today at one in the afternoon, just in time for
lunch. I woke up at eight and didn't know what to do with
myself. I woke up at nine. I woke up feeling bad as usual. I
woke up in a fury. I woke up this morning and pulled off the
sleep mask and the day was so bright. I woke up to the day
of my party, and at my party I was a little bored—I wished
there were more people there I wanted to impress, or who
scared me, or who had things in their lives that seemed
glamorous to me, rather than all these people I knew so
well. I woke up with a smile on my face and I was still smiling at the train station. I woke up without children. I won. I
wonder if he and I will argue for two or three more years,
and then there will be something good. I wonder if I wanted

to be a writer because nobody ever told me what the hell was going on, because nobody ever told me the truth. I wonder if I will get pregnant this year. I wonder if that's what life is going to be—a gradual process of moving away from all the things which seemed to promise a centre. I wonder if the beginning of a friendship is the optimistic waiting for something bad to happen, which can be overcome together, at which point the real friendship can begin. I wondered if this was what I patterned my love on, this feeling of scarcity which I have always had. I wore my new scarf and stockings, my boots from Paris, my navy blue dress, my spring coat, and I bought a set of hairbands which I would have liked to have been wearing earlier at the shoot, or at least I could have thought to put a bit of lipstick on. I worry that he is too much like my father, and that things will grow stale as they did with Pavel. I worry that he's like Mom, or will make me like Mom, or that I'm going to suffer too much. I worry there will not be enough people to collaborate with, or enough arteries from this place to carry my work elsewhere. I would go crazy if he fucked other women. I would have enjoyed having him here, reading beside me, and to have him touch me gently—or not—and to drink vodka together, or not. I would have to walk forty-five minutes in the beating sun up the mountain into the town just to check my email. I would like to be not at all biological, but that would be too dry a life. I would like to know life's laws. I would like to open up the universe, particularly the human universe and the human heart. I would like to think about consciousness and God these next few years. I would love to become a theoretical physicist. I would love to know some concrete things about the world. I would often rather lie in bed and think and feel than read. I wrote an email to Rosa this morning and received a beautiful letter from Lemons.

                                                                    Ice

cream was served. Ida criticizes herself for always defining herself in relation to a man, and I said that I had wasted too much of my life thinking about men, too. Ida didn't feel loved by him. Ida is smart about so much stuff, but she is not so smart about other people's feelings. Ida keeps saying that she thinks the person she ends up with will be somebody she already knows. Ida said that I could bring a TV over to her apartment and we could watch the movie there, but I wasn't sure how I would bring a TV set over. Ida told me over the phone that it was because she liked doers, not thinkers, after which Lemons asked me whether he was a doer or a thinker, but I wasn't sure. If I am right about this, I could also be wrong. If I could only win Pavel back—what a simple love we had!—but it's dying, as he says, it's dying now. If I found someone with whom it worked sexually and emotionally and intellectually—but maybe I'm not looking for this, maybe it's too soon or too threatening still, because then I really would be bonded with that person for life. If I had not had those two years of experiences with him, then it would not have been so hot when he came in my mouth, holding my head so I had no choice but to take it, though when he released his grip I tried discreetly to spit it out, and ended up leaking it from my lips onto the hem of Laurel's pretty dress, which she had worn to host the party that night, and had asked me if she should wear the night before. If I think about my romantic life, it has progressed the way some other people, perhaps dissatisfied, have allowed their work to progress: by way of habit, the demands of others, escapism, spur of the moment, and default. If I want to write, I have to move away from, not towards, the dazzle. If I went back to him now, I would feel stifled, I know I would, and I would still be in the same place, and I would make the same decisions, and I'd break up with him again. If in ten years I have a personality, that will be nice. If it comes, it will come in its own time and in its own clothes. If Lars sees me as a burden, that doesn't mean I am one. If my life becomes a complete and loveless mess, I can always kill myself or do a lot of other things. If part of what it means to be a human is not to have many experiences, but to have one perpetual experience of the self which never ceases, then it's best to stop performing to know who you truly are and look yourself flush in the face. If that means lying in bed all day, then that is what I will do. If this book is any good, it will be because of a concentration of mental energy, even in times when you didn't know where you were going. If you are living a horrible, valueless, degenerate life, the life of a bourgeois pig, so be it. If you are so great, why does no one like what you make? If you are too afraid to call him, you should be too afraid to go on a date with him, or to have sex with him. If you cannot love the ugliness that comes from within you, then you cannot make art. If you go into the deepest, most base feeling inside yourself, which is the fundamental feeling that doesn't change, then you can start writing and continue writing from there, for that is the feeling that is most fundamentally you, which maybe most calls upon to be expressed. If you hold fiercely to your vision, you will be protected. If you're too conservative, the tide will come and it will knock you down. In a very quiet way, this was one of the most amazing days of my life. In his text message, Pavel sent me a kiss for my knee, one for my arm—I was stung by a bee—and one for my cheek. In life, the remainder is always zero. In many cases, someone could be evil, or could be possessed by the devil and not want to be possessed, or could be going to hell or already *be* in hell, or it could all be a dream, or as the man on the streetcar said, *maybe we are all being controlled at this moment by evil forces, and sex is half a sin, isn't it?* In my case, I clutter my head and my life with men who I imagine are, or who actually are, emotionally dependent on me, and I simply clutter my life with people, all of whom I feel I need to escape from in order to write, just like I did when I was a child, but I was better at closing my door then. In my dream last night, I kept leaving my computer everywhere, losing it and coming back for it, thinking it was gone and then finding it again. In my dream last night, I understood myself to be a very beautiful and desirable woman. In my stomach, a river feeling, like there is something rushing or rumbling. In situations where I am suffering, it is worth asking whether I am making myself suffer, because it's probably often just a habit of mind. In some cases, being good to one person means being less good to another, different person. In that mother dream, I was shouting and screaming at her and crying hysterically, as I have never done in real life. In the autumn, electricity withdraws into the earth and rests. In the distance, a pale sky tinged with mauve. In the early hours of the morning there was the sound of prayers calling out over all of Istanbul, and I went out on the balcony and saw and watched the birds swooping around. In the morning, a loud, low-flying jet cut across the sky and everyone on the street looked up. In the morning, an email from Lemons—he is getting married. In the taxi, Vig played with his phone and I was a little taken aback. In truth, everything decays at the same rate. Including this little ugly boy with the British face who keeps running back and forth. Instead of giving yourself rules and orders, why not reason with yourself? Instead of going on the internet, why not ask the difficult questions of yourself? Instead of wasting your life, you are really spending a lot of time polishing it, not wanting to break it. Is it enough to have a beautiful voice? Is that escapism, wanting to break up? Is that so wrong? Is that too romantic? Is that what the dream was saying? Is there a fundamental personality? Is this moving forward? Is this the heart or just your mind in a loop? Is this your better and best idea? Is this your only idea? Isn't grace sometimes granted? Isn't there something reassuring about not being adored? It all has to be worked out in the fiction. It all seems so exhausting and hard. It all seems so sad to me now. It always felt to me like my thoughts and feelings could harm other people. It always seemed to me that I was helpless before the unfolding. It does not give a single thing to my soul. It does not matter whether we can be forgiven; forgiveness means nothing because what caused us to behave that way is still inside us, and forgiveness does not touch the source of our behaviour, it will only happen again. It doesn't matter if I shower, for I cannot get the hospital off me, that mixture of astringent and creamed stew and soiled and washed linens, and vitamins pitched high and low. It feels better not to empty myself into other people. It feels good to ground myself. It feels good to work, and it feels good to have worked. It feels like a lonely life. It feels like I am underwater, unable to breathe, and when I try to breathe, it is just water that I'm breathing. It feels like my apprenticeship is over, is coming to an end. It feels like the end of a ten-year cycle. It feels like the storm has passed. It feels so good to have enough money. It feels so warm and comforting. It felt like a relief and I burst into tears. It felt like my life had already been lived, every moment of it, and nothing new would ever happen again; I felt this so keenly last night, sitting there in the kitchen while Pavel cooked. It felt like something in me was rising, like the basement was becoming the first floor. It gives me pleasure to wash my dishes and put them away, it gives me pleasure to eat food I find good, and to eat all day long, and it gives me pleasure to sit comfortably in a chair. It gives me pleasure to wear the right outfit and to see the apartment tidy, and it gives me no pleasure to wake up with words in my head already. It has always been this back-and-forth with him; it has always been this way with everybody. It has been a bad and sad time. It has been a hot summer. It has been so long since we made love. It is a great failure to age. It is a hot day, and when I got home, my underwear was sweating. It is a question of metabolism, writing, of being able to sit in one place for six or seven hours. It is a way of spending energy and throwing chaos and conflict into my life so I don't have to do the hard work of writing. It is already three p.m. It is amazing how easy it is and how it costs nothing to italicize something. It is amazing to me how much people read. It is an honourable thing and a wise decision not to speak about your relationships. It is annoying that it takes thirty years to be an adult. It is becoming very embarrassing. It is clear that I have spent these past three years thinking about myself, and that I have a gap in my education three years long. It is exhausting to get into relationships and out of them; you do not want that anymore. It is exhausting, dizzying. It is good to feel all sorts of things, even the bad things that scare you, because they, too, push you in the direction of your convictions. It is good training for the future—to show yourself how to relax about parties. It is good when little happens, because then everything can be taken in. It is great to get done all the things on your list of things to get done. It is hard not to project into the future, but if you do, you see a mirage, then the mirage becomes something you move towards or away from, and then you are living like a parched person hallucinating, stumbling through the desert. It is hard to feel anything, the older one gets. It is important to preserve your inner composure and not allow yourself to be swept along by the bustle of life. It is interesting that he still wants to teach her. It is intolerable! It is just pure fantasy. It is like the Kierkegaardian thing: the duty is to love, but love creates the duty. It is loss and change. It is loss and pain. It is nearly four in the morning. It is nearly two in the morning, essentially the thirtieth, but the day doesn't end until I fall asleep. It is never certain, never safe. It is nice to have a friend I can be jealous of. It is nice to think about the fact that just because things are hard, that doesn't mean they can't lead somewhere good—and I feel the possibility of a real happiness, not a temporary sort of happiness or insanity where I leave my relationship, then have to start my life all over again, and get a temporary lift from stirring everything up, but ultimately wind up back in much the same place that I started. It is not a life of the intellect. It is not that a relationship with him is wrong, it is that this relationship with him is wrong. It is now one in the morning. It is now the middle of the night. It is now three a.m. It is one of the tricks of art. It is only a matter of time before I cycle through every man I know. It is only his cheering at the TV that I find so strange. It is perhaps my brother who I love with the least complexity. It is really not sex that I'm after, so much as the diversion of the air of a love affair. It is so appealing to get to this place where there is such a variety of things being offered to you, this cheese, that cheese, this salami, fruit, some chocolates— they put out so much trying to please you. It is so beautiful. It is so hard to talk with Vig about things. It is so intensely painful when things are bad between us. It is starting to bore the hell out of me. It is strange being in a rich man's house. It is tedious, it brings comfort. It is the despair of one's life, being one's character, having one's characteristic pain, knowing who you are and seeing yourself for who you are, your limitations and whatever is tragic within you, which reveals itself despite your best intentions. It is the life of Montaigne I am thinking of—a best friend, a wife, a big house, an income and all the time writing. It is the only restaurant open in Donnini on a Sunday night. It is the rare, rare man whose body I completely like. It is this modest blue room downstairs. It is true what Lemons says about Rosa; that her humour is meant to deflate. It is two days before my period, so maybe things feel worse than they would feel at another time of the month, but I kind of doubt it. It is wanting to remain in a childlike state of powerlessness, while having the man be the omnipotent, the ego, the one who determines what is valuable and what is not. It just seems like I can't stay in Toronto forever or I would always be a child, always comfortable, always in high school or grade school or my childhood bedroom; always safe. It looks like there's going to be a big rain shower. It makes me feel like something is wrong with me when I don't work on my book, which is most days. It makes me feel scared and alone. It really is like an illness I didn't know I had. It reminds me of the ring that Mom used to wear when I was a child; that green stone with the gold. It seemed glamorous, sordid, honest and okay. It seems crazy to pay for stuffed cabbage. It seems hard to stay here with this history of pain built up. It seems impossible, but it's true. It seems like one of the conventions of novels are these exotic locations. It seems so beautiful to live with him and wake and go to sleep with him in different cities. It seems so easy to come back here, now that I'm not in New York, when New York felt so hard. It seems the main accomplishment now is to make a thing like a baby. It seems urgent and necessary. It should flow like ink from a pen. It should show the hole, the lack. It sounded like a sixteenth-century world. It struck me as absurd that I should be grovelling to be Lars's girl. It struck me as profoundly boring. It struck me at once as instantly absurd. It struck me that the reason I'd had two men in my mind all these years was maybe because I was scared that there would be no one to take care of me if my present relationship didn't work out, or perhaps it was this fantasy of an ideal caretaker— as if Lars could be a caretaker! It took me ages to get to

Adam Phillips's house, and it was hard to find but I found it, and he was very kind and I liked him right away. It was a beautifully sunny day. It was a brilliant morning, I could have read all day. It was a nice, warm night. It was a small beach, the size of a backyard. It was as if all the apples, all the stories, gave way to the season where there was only one apple. It was beautiful with the sun coming in, and the stone walls. It was dark and chaotic. It was during a blackout. It was erotic but also humiliating. It was fine, it was simple. It was grey and blue and dark and mysterious. It was just bourgeois adults with their orgies. It was near the end of the party, around two in the morning. It was nearly seven or eight and I was just starving. It was nice to get dressed in my new boots and jeans, and to pack a new sweater, with my haircut which everyone seemed to like, and no one noticing I had changed the colour; good. It was nice to step outside with him this morning as he smoked, and it was a little cold, it being October, and he and I walked down the street so I could give my rent cheque to my landlord, which was actually Agnes's cheque, written to my landlord, me not having enough money this month. It was night. It was only a month and a half ago that you believed that you and Lars would be waiting for each other! It was only five months ago that you were in New York, hanging out with Lemons. It was only two months ago that you thought you had found the man who ruined you for all other men. It was only when I put my hands together that I realized the burning in my hands could be relieved by bringing my hands together in prayer, and that maybe the burning was a sign that I must find my strength, not in writing, not in men, but in God. It was raining. It was so beautiful. It was so clear that I had made the right decision. It was so clear to me! It was so painful to see him cry and try to talk through his tears. It was the approach of winter that made me want to go somewhere cold, and that is why I thought of St. Petersburg. It was too careerist there. It was too much for me. It was true that when I woke the next morning, it wasn't as though the thought of him was in my head, but rather that my head was in the thought of him; the thought of him was bigger than my head. It was very flattering and my feathers puffed slightly. It will be a book for the future. It will be as calculated and controlled as the last book was instinctual and out of control. It will be as separate from my actual life as the last book was indivisible from it. It will be created through time, and it doesn't have to be about the nightmare in my soul. It will be fun, I hope. It will have an easy air. It will never be clear. It will not be fiction, and it will not tell a story, and there will be no characters, and you will not worry about the voice or the way it is written, just about what you are saying. It will not end the epoch. It will not work without the totality of your mind. It won't be done until February. It would be nice to be back in Eastern Europe, where I felt so at home; even the harsh edge the women had made sense to me, reminded me so much of my mother, that kind of brusqueness which North American women don't have so much, that brutality. It would be nice to get better at writing. It would be nice to make a little book of all the injunctions you have towards yourself. It wouldn't help me at all. It's 2:34 every time I check the time these days. It's 4 p.m. It's 4:41 now. It's a fantasy of being saved. It's a stupid idea. It's a yellow, cloudy sky. It's amazing to me how life keeps going. It's better to work, to go into the underground cave where there are books, than to fritter away time online. It's crazy that I need all of these mental crutches in order to live. It's fiction. It's fine. It's good to be without a partner now, for as Lemons said, *you can't really have a partner while you're writing this book, can you?* It's good to tie things up and get them out of my mind. It's hard as a diamond and wide, and I love that about his cock, and I never knew another cock like it till his. It's just a fact. It's just as Grandma said, *you cannot make someone love you who does not.* It's kind of amazing how only when I'm most broke and most out of prospects does money seem to come along. It's like being at my desk but the colours are reversed. It's like I don't even know how to behave, but I know in some instances how I want to behave, so maybe the times when I don't know how to behave are the times that don't really matter, and I don't have to worry about those. It's my last day here. It's my third peanuts party in a year! It's not clear to me that I am not some bottom-of-the-barrel writer, or whether I should trust the compliments of my friends, because can't everyone find friends to give them compliments? *It's not necessarily a position of disrespect to be the wife who is cheated on*, he said. It's not rational. It's not responsible. It's not right. It's not worth the sex if you have to put up with bad art. It's okay to be a coward. It's okay to describe the little pleasures of modern life, like the nice thing about a sandwich. It's okay. It's okay, whatever happens. It's okay, you can be happy. It's over. It's pathetic. It's pointless and it hurts everybody. It's true that when I tried to put his dick into me yesterday and he got a little soft, I was jumping the gun. It's what I do in any situation, no matter who I'm with. It's what I know how to do.

Jack said he would be happy to live in Toronto if he thought he could find a man here, but there are no men in this city, so he had to come to Berlin. Jack tried to pick up the man who left on the bicycle. Jack wandered over to the low stone wall by the river and lay there for a while. Jack was a rock star because he liked all of it, playing music, the reaction of the crowd, being up there performing. Jack was lying on the floor, too drunk to be sitting up. Jack was making out with three men. Jack was photographing himself with his computer, in black and white, moving his hand gradually across his face—an animation. Jack's certainty that he will eventually write more songs. Joseph and I got a room together and we went into the bathtub to wash our feet. Joseph and I went into the woods. Joseph and I were supposed to swim together tonight but I think neither of us wanted to; after a day in a car together, you'd rather be alone. Joseph and Jack are looking out the windows of the tour bus. Joseph bought Jack some falafel. Joseph is asleep on the sleeper with his beautiful brown hair all over his face. Joseph lay down at one point during the show and was covered in sweat and I had a desire to lick him. Joseph only reads *Steppenwolf.* Joseph picked up a man on the street in Madrid and they spent twenty minutes in the basement of that man's apartment, getting it on. Joseph said he doesn't want to sing Jack's fucking music in the fucking tour van because that only validates it. Joseph said he prefers the smaller shows because he can go and do merch after and meet the crowd; he does not like the big stadium shows because there you cannot. Joseph said he was shitting blood for three days after Jack fucked him without lube and without a condom, the first time they met and had sex. Joseph said, *in your position? I wouldn't have come.* Joseph says, *it's funny that Jack says he's looking for love, when he's one of the least loving people I know.* Joseph wanted to explore Barcelona but we were too drunk on gin and tonics. Joseph was saying that he was deeply ambivalent about his relationship with his boyfriend, because he doesn't think he would choose this man as his friend, and he thought it would be much nicer to have a boyfriend he could have an intellectual connection with, someone with opinions—who wasn't, as he put it, *so much a part of the herd.* Just as some ideas must be accepted many times, other ideas must be rejected many times. Just be quiet and retain your dignity and think about how everyone has their own image of goodness, and you have to remain close to yours or else your life will be a complete blur, mud, a mess, a mistake. Just because he has the courage to ruin his life and sell his soul, doesn't mean I must do that, too. Just because there are difficulties, that doesn't mean you have done anything wrong. Just because things are hard, that doesn't mean you made the wrong decision. Just deprive that part of your brain, deprive it of oxygen and let it die. Just don't think about it. Just kidding.

Keep a list of all the people you need to speak to, and read the books you need to read. Keep good track of your receipts. Keep in mind that none of these projects will make you any money. Keep it in a container, and publish only what has reached the next stage of accomplishment. Keep the energies in your body and contain them. Keep the house clean and neat, love him, love family and friends. Keep this paragraph which will ruin the whole entire thing. Keep this paragraph, this ugly worm that will eat all the papers and destroy it. Keep your eye on the distant, distant justification for all this. Killing evil thoughts. Knew it would only last a day. Knocked out my tooth this morning and can't find my gold coin. Know how to love a man by knowing how to love writing. Know there is always an alternative to the situation, even being very babyish and all alone.

L ars and I went into the woods. Lars cannot be with me. Lars could have called me at any time today. Lars doesn't answer my emails. Lars doesn't listen to you or pay attention to you or even let you speak. Lars doesn't love you in that way. Lars doesn't want a life with you. Lars doesn't want to be with you for all of the many reasons I have not wanted to be with men, and I never thought of those men, *well, if they had done this a little differently or not done that, things would have been different,* but rather that things might have been somewhat different, but they would have come to the same ultimate end. Lars fucked the girl at one-thirty and they met at one. Lars had his head resting on my belly, his legs around my legs, and I had one hand on his head. Lars had never been so angry at me before, and I was never convinced he cared all that much, but when I saw how I had hurt him, I was surprised, for I obviously mean more to him than I thought. Lars has absolute power and I have none, and he doesn't reply to my emails, and I am unable to reach him because his phone is broken. Lars has become unenthusiastic in his contact with me since leaving here yesterday. Lars has been holding himself apart from me, which is hard. Lars has been just as secretive, just as guarded, and just as unreliable as he was all summer, telling me that his girlfriend is going to Mexico with him, then in the next email saying, *or maybe not*. Lars is a beautiful man. Lars is not going to write me back, either because he is a selfish and uncaring person, or because I'm a bad and selfish person. Lars is not interested in being your boyfriend or your husband, ever. Lars is not interested in you. Lars is not superior to any man. Lars is not superior to any of my friends. Lars is reticent and secretive and private. Lars is self-absorbed and self-pitying. Lars is so beautiful and I love having him in bed with me. Lars is so truly not in love with me. Lars is the sort who will always leave. Lars once told me that it would scare women how much he thought about fucking other women. Lars only excited the female parts of me, while the male parts of me weren't into him, didn't like him, didn't respect him. Lars passed me his phone; there had been a choir on the streetcar earlier and he had recorded it on his phone. Lars peered in, squinting, touching my cheeks, and said he couldn't see anything, no blood. Lars pulled my hair, grabbed me. Lars put his hands on me and led me into a corridor. Lars really does combine all the characteristics I most feel I need in a man. Lars replied to my text without any real love, and twice he got off the phone quickly. Lars said he didn't like it because it made him feel like a sex toy, to come into bed and have me pull off his clothes and want to fuck. Lars said that he wants to be single and that he wants to be with lots of girls, girls in Mexico. Lars said that in Los Angeles, people only want to know whether you're in the film business or whether they're going to fuck you. Lars said, *I paid for your ice cream—that's that.* Lars said, *you live the way a mammal should, according to your instincts.* Lars seemed to me, on first sight, like a man with a loose and easy morality, a loose and easy attitude towards life, someone who has never had to try very hard, doing things simply and without much care. Lars thought it might be best not to say what qualities he wanted in a woman. Lars touched my face in the cab. Lars wants to be with a regular girl who is not an artist, who will cook for him, he says. Lars was beautiful and I tried to persuade him not to go. Lars was rude to someone who bought the art. Lars was so loving to me last night at the gallery. Lars was talking about theatre or something, and I realized that I was bored with his interests. Lars was up in my mind from reading *Lady Chatterley's Lover*, finishing it this morning around seven. Last night at the party I told him I had big news, and he suddenly turned red and asked me if I was pregnant. Last night he took me and pulled me close to him and looked down into my face. Last night he was saying how he liked how my face was female, but also male. Last night he was talking about how bad he had been, a drunk, getting thrown in jail, drinking a hundred bottles of wine, getting into fights. Last night I had dinner with him, but I got nervous right at the end in case there would be a romantic moment, which I did not want. Last night I had some new thoughts, for his question was about what I liked about being in a relationship, and I'd answered him in all the usual ways, but then when I looked into my own heart as I lay in bed and couldn't sleep, I saw that what a relationship was maybe most about for me was my desire to subjugate myself under somebody. Last night I made him walk down the street as though he didn't know me. Last night I read through old letters. Last night I sort of felt this twinge of sadness or loss or loneliness when Pavel and I were coming down from the second floor with drinks, and I was implying that he should come to the front of the stage with me to watch Laurel give her speech, and he gestured and said, *I'm going over there*, and I realized it was to his new girlfriend. Last night I was on Criticker for several hours. Last night it didn't really work, and Pavel explained that he thought that Gestalt therapy had kind of ruined him for sex, because Gestalt is all about looking at yourself looking at yourself looking at yourself looking at yourself as a child. Last night we shared a pizza. Last night we talked a little more openly about sex, then Fiona went down on me. Last night we went out for a walk and in a very natural way we ended up in a gelato shop. Last night, high, I didn't know how to think of him; at times I was incredibly delighted and thought he was about as new and perfect as a person could possibly be; at other times I found it impossible to understand why I was with someone who insulted me, was unkind, and made me feel insecure. Last night, walking in the streets after the movie, I felt so different in relation to other humans, not inferior or superior, but as though we were all members of the same species. Lately I have been noticing something strange with the older people I know, writers I look up to; part of me wonders whether I should bother getting close to them if they are going to die. Later he cut a piece of bread for me and our fingers accidentally touched when he handed me the slice. Later I lay there holding him, my head curled into his chest, and I was filled with a great feeling of pleasure and delight. Laughter from the hotel window was falling into the street, rolling through the gutters. Laying in bed and considering different possible contexts, it occurred to me how different I actually am from how I imagine myself to be. Leave something nice for him;

maybe you can buy groceries tomorrow or clean his fridge or something. Leave the pleasures of looking at the food on the supermarket shelves for tomorrow night, when there will be nothing to do, when he will be gone. Lemons asked if Ida would make a good wife, and I said I thought so because she seems very supportive. Lemons asked me why Rosa was single at this age, and I explained that it was perhaps because she was drawn to needy men, but these men could not be good in the world, could not be strong, and in the end they hurt or disappointed her, but that this was her instinct—I didn't know if she knew this—to go towards people in need. Lemons at times felt contemptuous of her, but never enough to corrupt his admiration, because there is too much there to admire, he says. Lemons doesn't really love her, he just thinks he does, or is saying he does, or acts like he does out of a sense of duty or guilt. Lemons feels that Ida made him a man. Lemons had been juggling his girlfriend that week, plus a woman he was having an affair with, telling me about both of them, wondering which of the two women he'd end up with, and apparently I'd said, *you're going to lose them both*. Lemons had to leave because she was coming straight from the airport—the woman he told me about two months ago. Lemons has a masculinity that I didn't at first see. Lemons has been counting the days since her last period, and he is really scared she's pregnant; he says they both need to make twenty thousand more a year before having a kid. Lemons has no feelings of guilt over ending the relationship because, he says, he gave while he was in it as much as he could possibly give. Lemons is a romantic, looking for his Eve. Lemons is all lit up with new confidence, given to him by the homeopath. Lemons is back with his girlfriend who he cheated on three times. Lemons is certain that they will get back together, that he's the man for her, and that she needs to think things through, figure things out, and then she will return to him. Lemons is consumed with Ida; believes that he has ruined his life and that now he will never find love. Lemons is looking forward to wooing some girl in California. Lemons is losing his hair, I think, with all the stress of the last six months, perhaps some of the blond has gone out of it, too. Lemons is unreliable but perhaps a real friend. Lemons just broke up with her—that lasted a month, maybe two. Lemons last night marvelled about how many chances one got—he got—at having a good life. Lemons missed his chance in February. Lemons moved to Paris for seven years and now he is back here, adjusting. Lemons never wanted to have children before, but now he does. Lemons put his arm over the back of her seat, half-turned around, and made a kind of gesture like, *tell me more*. Lemons really seems to be in love with Ida. Lemons rejected my book, and when my agent told me this, I felt happy for some reason. Lemons said all of his best relationships have been the ones in which he was the pursuer. Lemons said he didn't want to take the smallest step in the direction of jeopardizing what they have, which doesn't mean that he's not attracted to other women. Lemons said he wished they could get all the romance and seduction over with and just settle down to being comfortable with each other. Lemons said not to publish the book if I was uncomfortable with it. Lemons said of his relationship with her, *that drove me crazy*. Lemons said, *it's a real courtesy to interrupt someone who's telling you a story if you've heard it before*. Lemons said, *pity the man who gets everything he wants*, and I said, *pity especially the man who gets everything he wants all in one night*. Lemons said, *publish it*, but I knew it wasn't right. Lemons said, *yeah, you two have little Jew-crushes on each other*. Lemons saying that I shouldn't have said that about Ida. Lemons says that Claire doesn't have normal conversations with people so she doesn't know how to write dialogue. Lemons says that he was numb these past three years. Lemons says that people will one day look back on Brooklyn the way they did on Paris. Lemons seems to like small, cute women, so he can enfold himself over them, not women his own size, or with an assertive voice who can look him in the face, like Rosa, who is not coy and seductive in that way. Lemons should break up with her already. Lemons smiled and said he knew. Lemons spoke to me for ten minutes about the love problems of a woman I don't even know. Lemons talked openly about being willing to break up with her in order to have five or ten more years without kids. Lemons thinks I need a new project, a big project, one that is more ambitious than the other ones—and longer—to occupy my days until I have a kid. Lemons thought that tutoring made more sense than hairdressing. Lemons told me he walked around in a fog for a year, couldn't think, couldn't look at women, did nothing. Lemons told me, lying in the grass, not to worry; that he could see me, sometimes when I turned around and walked away—that he'd catch a glimpse of my future self, and he said that I probably would be, when my restless sexuality settled down, a grand sort of woman. Lemons wanted her, thinking she would fix him, but what he found instead was a strong person, while he was a weak one, and then he didn't want to be with her anymore. Lemons wanted the whole table to share, and Ida wanted everyone to have their own plate, but really, she just wanted her own plate. Lemons wants to marry her; he sounds like an idiot whenever he describes her. Lemons was devastated by this appraisal. Lemons was emotionally frigid and couldn't love a woman, he would always come to think there was a better woman out there and become remote. Lemons was probably confused and feeling guilty, having received a package from another girl. Lemons was saying that both of his exes criticized him for wanting a relationship in which he could take them for granted. Let all the fragments of life die away. Let everything inessential die. Let life happen as it did back then, when you weren't so afraid, so intent on preserving, so afraid of everything crumbling to the ground. Let my mother kill me, let anyone kill me. Let the books gallivant in the warmth of Spain, while you stay at your desk, writing. Let the novelists write the novels. Let the past be the past and move forward. Let the work be your only voice. Let this be the impulse under which you write it: sentence follows sentence, truth follows truth. Let time do its job. *Let's sit here*, he said, and we sat beneath a Godot-like tree, small. Life feels like a wonderful neutrality these days. Life is long so growth can happen slowly, but I always want it to happen all at once. Life is so hard and it never ends. Life seems to be next year in Barcelona, with him. Like a bird moving from flower to flower, you will just move to another flower. Like a good-looking girl. Like a little abortion of something. Like a little kid running after a train. Like a table with four legs. Like I cut off one head and another grows somewhere else. Like our brains are not powerful enough, not smart enough, not taking in enough, to do all the things we want. Like Radiguet says, the very suppression of one's eccentricity is what makes the work brilliant. Like this morning he was making zucchini-nut-chocolate-chip muffins at six a.m., and eventually I got up and went to sit with him in the kitchen while he did. Live in the truth of life—in the reality. Live where there is truth, in the realm of the actual. Loneliness after Lemons's wedding. Loneliness is not the end. Look at all the books I have. Look, I am nearly thirty! Looking at Craigslist apartments in Hungary, I thought, *I do not want to move to Budapest.* Looking at the toilet, I thought, *that can't be; life is meaningful in itself, and your work is meaningful because you do it.* Looking out the living room window which was covered in vines. Losing Lars as the centre of my life. Lots of people reach out to old lovers in this state. Lots of women want him, and you are the same.

Make enough money to live. Make him feel loved and special. Make sure you buy warmer boots. Make sure you have breakfast. Make sure you publish another theatre review. Making money. Making out with the anti-neo-Nazi girl, who confided that the anti-neos had no chance against the neos, for the neos have better self-discipline and are not always taking drugs and getting drunk, are not undisciplined and lazy. Marriage and divorce as a rite of passage. Marriage can make misery more bearable. Marriage is one step closer to divorce than being in a relationship. Marriage will not settle my restlessness. Maybe Agnes has had better boyfriends than me, although I don't know them from the inside side of intimacy. Maybe all the things I think about longingly, that I seem unable to do—be a certain kind of person in a loving relationship, and so on—are dormant potentials in me, whereas the things we don't fantasize about would be more likely to shut us down. Maybe art is too dangerous for me. Maybe go to Montreal for a month. Maybe have a goal in mind so time is not wasted. Maybe he was right when he said I could only ever be happy with a man who degrades me. Maybe he was tired when he got home and he didn't know how to put all of his complicated thoughts into an email. *Maybe he's not your life partner*, Claire said. Maybe I am beginning to feel humbled, seeing people younger than me with so much success, and people my age, too, living lives that seem so glamorous, whose writing is so different from mine. Maybe I can get what I need in other ways, Rosa suggested. Maybe I can watch *Manhattan* with him one last time in bed. Maybe I could write a novel with sentences and characters in it. Maybe I really am just a loner. Maybe I should do it alone. Maybe I should not talk to anybody. Maybe I will see Rosa for tea. Maybe I would grow tired of it, but right now, the idea of having sex every day with a man like Lars, or Lars himself, seems good. Maybe I'll get my nails done at some point. Maybe I'll have a party in New York in January and invite Claire and a bunch of my friends. Maybe I'll wait thirty or forty years to be interviewed. Maybe if one gets sick of it, it ends. Maybe it will be nice to really think about things for a change; something is preventing me from thinking right now, a kind of anxiety or fear, I don't know.

Maybe it's like finding writing, something so endless. Maybe my fantasies for my life are those of a much younger person, who hadn't yet become this person, or was on her way to becoming someone else but ended up as this person, and no longer needs to pin her girlish hopes on frail or too-simplistic fantasies, like some Madame Bovary. Maybe my twenties were about writing and finding a man, and my thirties will be about being with him and learning how to write. Maybe nobody's life is any different from that. Maybe one day you'll be called away and you'll go, but for now you're here, and you have to be here or else you're not really here. Maybe talk to religious people and see if it's so—that there is no gap, or if there is, is it adequately filled by God? Maybe that is what Ellis meant about art; that it rekindles itself. Maybe that is what is making me nauseous. Maybe that is when he stopped trusting me or wanting to be with me or sleep with me, and maybe that's when I became scared and stopped trusting him, and perhaps that's when our conflicts began. Maybe that's just paranoid. Maybe there are these little windows where you can change your life utterly, and if you don't take them, the opportunity for change passes. Maybe this is just how I always feel in November. Maybe this is why some loves work and others don't, why sometimes two people find each other and it's like the easiest thing in the world to fall into, and they miss each other and feel an absence when the other isn't around; something about a harmony, like the two sides of the brain. Maybe when I'm older and much more famous, people will do for me the stupid things they do for the famous. Meanwhile I am trying to have one ugly video of me from Sydney taken down from the internet. Meanwhile she writes her increasingly hysterical and meaningless books and she has become impossible to be around. Meeting the same people you knew ten years ago and seeing how much worse you've all become, more dull, more cynical about each other, less pleasant to be around. Men always seemed so threatening, like they would be like vines and choke me, would twist themselves around my hands and wrists and I would get no work done. Midday has come and the sun shines in with a bright yellow light. Midnight. Miss my brother. Mom and I fought because she wouldn't let me eat a slice of pizza in the car. Mom and I went to the jewelry store. Mom called this morning and said she compromised happiness in her marriage in order to fulfill the one thing she would not compromise on, her work. Mom has changed so much, she has so much more of a sympathetic and loving nature than she ever had, and a much more ironic and humourous relation to herself and the world. Mom just came out into the hall where I was writing, and now she's going to the bathroom in another part of the hotel to take pictures of whatever she finds there. Mom on the phone yesterday said how impressed she was the last time she saw me, how grown-up I appeared, and that I really seemed to know in what direction I wanted to go in, and that I spoke so articulately and intelligently. Mom said she can't really respect someone who hasn't worked hard and made something of themselves. Mom said, *some women want Brad Pitt—that doesn't mean they can have him.* Monday I worked all day at the café and then read the Baldwin and did my emails. Money always comes; it comes when you are true. Money is a problem for all of us. Mos Def has a house in Toronto. Mostly these days I'm just lying in bed. Must a person always be expanding themselves? Must go and study under a master. Must tell him to stop emailing me. Must we sing about beautiful things? Must we suffer till the end of history? My apprenticeship in art and my apprenticeship in romance. My arms were rigid. My bleached white hair. My body chose him, no one else's did. My body was so primed for him. My book for all the people. My book is going badly. My book suddenly makes sense. My book will be done this year! My brain has turned itself off. My brain is catching up with me in its exhaustion. My brain is like the viscous stuff around a brain—that's where it's located, in the slippery goo between the two hemispheres, between the brain itself and the skull; whatever the viscous substance is, that is where my brain is located and where my soul is, too. My brain still feels fried after smoking up with Piper last night. My computer is getting increasingly slow. My courage had been circumstantial. My dream of leaving all this behind and just having a family in Montreal, and writing only if I feel like it but not to make money, whereas now it has become a profession and I am so conscious of having to make something good, and to be good, and all the chatter if one is not good or has done something bad, and all the expectations. My duty to sitting in a room and becoming a certain kind of writer—yet when I look at that future, it seems so bleak, competing in the marketplace and whatnot. My hair is pulled back in a ponytail. My head wants to explode. My heart feels cold towards him. My heart is light again, and all that I was going to write about death seems to have vanished. My initial point and what I meant to say was that every situation is different, and I'm realizing that you cannot avoid unhappiness, and you cannot avoid pain, and you cannot make rules and live by them in order to create a happy life, for I really think that leads to a life of total isolation from other people and experiences, because of course it's other people and experiences that bring you pain. My jaw is tight and I feel like I'm going to cry—why does he keep me waiting, making me suffer? My life feels a little better since talking about it with Rosa. My life feels great. My loneliness can be attributed to Pavel, yes, but more particularly to me not working. My main wish for life right now is not to think about men all the time, but to ever more think about men less and less, and to look around at the world, and at my books, and at the books I want to write and the work I want to do, and get over my neuroses about everything, and stop smoking and feel my own will, which is my soul, and to have some control over how I react, and to be in the world in a more thoughtful way, and to come out of childhood and be a woman at last. My middle finger is still hurting from when I slammed it in the door. My mind is back with Lars since his email of last night in which he suggested that he might move to the city for me. My mind was racing with all these thoughts, and I asked myself if these thoughts were good, and my mind said no.

Neglect my friends and family. Never having felt so sad. New sheets for the bed. New York, I think, made me depressed. Nice after we were done to lie there holding him, but at a certain point it became too much, and that is when I had to leave. Nine years later, almost the exact same thing. No checking email on Sunday. No justification is needed. No kiss at all. No love is perfect. No matter how nice or interesting these people are, it doesn't feel worth the trouble. No matter what direction I went in, I would probably always have some suspicion of myself, some criticisms. No more controlling. No more Facebook. No more mysticism, or not so much. No more playing a part. No more second-guessing. No more stupid assignments. No more Twitter. No need to worry about leaving town; think always of Glenn Gould. No one at this point in history knows how to live, so we read biographies and memoirs, hoping to get some clues. No one can take away the simple happiness and pleasure I get from my life in Toronto. No one else knows my plan. No one even said thanks. No one sees, no one applauds. No one thinks you're so great. No phone, no internet. No place I need to go. No point worrying. No rules for my life. No union is without its blank spaces. Nobody can promise that their feelings won't change. Nobody knows why marriages happen. None of this comes out of anxiety or neuroses. None of this is causing the smallest flurry of feeling in me. None of this is very interesting to read, I'm afraid, and I know it won't be interesting for me to read later. Nor do I even turn to books for that. Not a man who shows signs of vulnerability, unlike some men, who seem to me entirely vulnerability. Not always being jealous, not always feeling like an outsider. Not being in reality, which is here and now. Not boys or writing or being supercute. Not buying expensive presents for people. Not casual or posing. Not decadent, narcissistic, meaningless or vain. Not drinking alcohol, coffee or even black tea. Not during the mornings or most of the day. Not enough brains to distribute among us humans. Not enough girls in my week. Not enough sleep. Not everybody needs a home with other people. Not everybody needs a spouse and children. Not everyone does, but that's part of the reason for her success. Not everything is for the best, nor should it be, and it's impossible to even know what *for the best* means, given that we do not know what life is or its purpose. Not having rules and not having obstructions. Not having to poll everyone before I do something, nor having to ask anyone for their permission. Not just intercourse, but real desire. Not just the fact that a person can make a wish, but that a person is given three. Not maroon, which is too brown. Not me, because I'm leaving town. Not perfectionism. Not quite. Not replying to my comment about breaking up with him. Not smoking cigarettes. Not spending money adds energy to your art. Not the movie-makers, not the fashion designers, not the chefs. Not thinking about advancing in the world, but rather in your consciousness and your work. Not to be a waste of a life. Not to be impatient with myself or my insides. Not to be so swayed by him. Not to live according to images, but according to time. Not to live according to story, but according to feelings. Not to make him or any other man into a god, nor to make God into a man. Not to say that you should live a monkish life without a partner or other humans, but do remember what you are wedded to. Not to talk to Rosa about my romantic life anymore, for she is too influential, the things she says. Not to use the book as an excuse for anything anymore, for there will always be a book. Not to worry about sentences. Not to worry about timeliness. Not wanting painful feelings. Not wanting to fill the void with men. Not-smart boys are no fun to be around. Nothing feels on the verge of revealing itself; nothing is on the cusp of being new. Nothing really happened this month. Now all of a sudden I feel a longing for Pavel. Now all the men I liked most are lost to me, and all the men of lesser importance as well. Now he is gone and I feel fine. Now I am drinking tea. Now I am feeling like shit. Now I am getting tired, so I will write one more story and then go to bed. Now I am not living honestly again. Now I am reading fiction. Now I am thinking about my book, and how it was all on track until Pavel said the other night, *maybe if it had some emotion in it, your seven-hundred-page book might actually be worth reading.* Now I come to the part of the night that I don't want to write about, because I began to get drunk, and I woke up this morning feeling shame and regret. Now I feel like I want to cry. Now I feel terrible and he does, too. Now I have a miserable day ahead of me because of our stupid fight. Now I see that he has not sent me any sweet texts or replied to my email, probably because he feels the reassurance I need, and which I am trying to extract from him. Now I think it's pretty funny. Now I think: if my romantic life was more stable, my writing life might become more unpredictable and adventurous. Now I want to write books forever. Now I wonder if that's what sanity is—what the man on the streetcar said—just having a game in your head. Now I'm back to this? Now it is later in the summer. Now it is one in the morning. Now it would make sense to read and educate myself—to see the landscape around me and what other people are doing. Now it's a story: a girl is looking for herself, abandoning art, looking for ways out, trying to find ways of living that are art-like but not art, but she can't find the answer of how to make art that is not art at home, so she travels around the world to try and figure it out, but nothing is happening there either, then her mother calls and asks for her help in cleaning out her basement, so she returns and is broke and so starts working in a hair salon where she meets a hairdresser who becomes a role model of professionalism and mastery, and she realizes this is what she wants to be—a master of her craft—so she quits the salon and returns to art with the knowledge of where, how and in what direction to go. Now my whole body is cold, very cold. Now that my book is done, I must starve or asphyxiate the part of my brain that thinks about the book. Now that the book is done, I can commit to him, I think. Now that the book is done, I need not panic about anything. Now the idea spins into hubris. Now the sky is the colour of computers. Now you are believing another cultural myth, which has no basis in the facts of life as you have seen them.

Of course I had images of me in Florence, walking in the light air in my new shoes and lying under a tree and studying physics. Of course I'm jealous of his girlfriend, and that he wants to be with someone like her, whoever she is, and not me. Of course in every happiness there is a tremendous blindness. Of course it was a joke. Of course it's nice to be invited up. Of course she pointed out that with me thinking about men all the time, it didn't leave enough of my brain for writing. Of course the sex, which is undeniable. Of course there's a lot of bad I'm overlooking, but we hugged and said hello with such chemistry and warmth and good feelings. Of course there's a ton of pleasure in it for me. *Of course they're sexy,* Hanif said, *and there seems to be something inside them you can't reach, but in fact it's just emptiness.* Of course this could be read by him as a pre-break-up email, but I didn't believe it was, I just wanted to know how it would feel to be apart from him and not in the mire of this confusion and doubt and craziness. Of course we have so much peace together. Of course you could try to relax with him, rather than stoking this feeling that things are always ending. Of course Zadie Smith is married. Of waking up in the morning and not knowing who you are and not needing to know. Oh, I feel so young and free of my book! Oh, look how beautiful he looks playing Scrabble! Oh, my beautiful man. On Friday, I'll be where it's simple, back at the salon. On one level I'm skeptical and on another I'm lazy; skeptical about whether it will make a difference, literature, and the skepticism and the laziness will marry each other and will probably prevent me from fulfilling my potential as a writer, but I don't know, sometimes I think about what Gil once said, that no one wants to read the work of an A+ student. On some level I should be alone right now, but on the other hand, one is always alone. On the drive to the airport, the sun comes out, and Amandine says, *now that you are leaving Paris, the sun comes out!* On the other hand, it may just be that all the things which in the past would have frustrated me and made me unhappy are precisely the things in my new life that I would find happiness in. On the other hand, it's good to have no money if I want to work harder, because then I've got two excuses not to go out so much. On the streetcar on my way to the hospital, an attractive boy was looking at me. On top of that, I had been sitting in the bathroom downstairs and looking in the mirror across from me and at *Vanity Fair* magazine, and thinking about whether or not I was beautiful, and about how this was not a reason to go to New York: to find out whether I'm beautiful. On Wednesday I got up and I had a tremendous feeling of happiness in me, and I went to Chelsea and saw art in the morning, and went to Williamsburg and bought clothes in the afternoon. One can't really relax in the midst of all these men. One could put the computer anywhere; it doesn't have to go on the desk. One could sit anywhere. One day, when things are other than they are right now, I will wonder why I wanted to leave this time so quickly, as I now wonder the same thing about the past. One feels one's own decay and it's hard to believe it's not visible and a turn-off. One has to be an artist and a warrior, both. One has to have the will to run absolutely roughshod over people. One has to let these evil time conditions pass. One has to slow down slightly in order to do this kind of work. One is in a relationship with something bigger than oneself. One is lucky to find people to persist with. One must see down to the depths; what is its ugliness, what is its beauty? One must start small—start beyond the self. One new thing happened yesterday; I began wearing lipstick because since I cut my hair men haven't been looking at me on the street, and I didn't like it, and when I told this to Rosa, she said, *start wearing lipstick*. One of the images she had was of a diamond, and how people get fixated on one or two of its facets, and never turn it around to see the other sides. One person is as good as the next, but then there are some people you are bound to, and for whatever reason they feel like destiny, or like some half-remembered dream, and one should just submit to those relationships and remain at peace. Only now, becoming ever more in relation to others, and not feeling the same unreality I always used to feel, am I starting to have human feelings, not just awe and terror like prehistoric man. Only the artists change your soul—that's the only thing they change—but the souls change everything else. Opening the side door of the apartment today and coming into the bedroom, I had a thought I'd never had before: *who cares if I am not with the perfect guy for me, or exactly the right man?* Or anyway, it was some position that was foreign to me. Or anyway, that I have given the wrong place in my life to relationships, and better that they are at the periphery, or happen out of the corner of my eye. Or be involved with men in a way that isn't about giving them everything, while simultaneously taking everything back, but instead give only what's appropriate to be given. Or maybe it was perfect, maybe it was okay. Or maybe it's a route to some other kind of writing. Or maybe there is so much inner life, it's unnecessary to get it from the people around you. Or maybe this will finally be the book without characters. Or one could say happiness, joy, liberation and beauty. Or perhaps it's too grand to speak of having emotions; what does it matter, one's emotions? Our empathy is frail. Our end is doom. Our relationship in miniature is his checking of a text message on his phone while I am baring my heart.

P aperback book was published. Paperback tour, eleven days. Papers upon papers. Paragraphs are pauses, chapters are also pauses. Part of her was breathless from feeling so alone. Part of her was suffering from knowing that she, for the first time in her life, wanted to stay. Part of what I dislike about her is her condescending, oblivious, professorial manner, as though she has a kindergarten lesson to teach everyone. Patricia Highsmith lost her virginity at Yaddo. Pavel admitted that Laurel was more sexual on the surface than I am, more of the flesh and always talking about sexual liberation and free love, but, he said, mocking her, *yeah, I've read all those books, too.* Pavel and I are on the train at Niagara Falls where we have been sitting stationary for an hour as the customs officers lead their dogs through. Pavel and I fought a lot in October. Pavel and I had a fight in the middle of the night after I yelled out to flush the toilet and he yelled back that he didn't like me yelling it. Pavel and I have been in a bad place since Sunday night. Pavel and I have been so exhausted lately. Pavel and I talked this weekend up at his sister's house and figured out the source of some of the problems between us. Pavel and I walked around the city today and told each other, *I'll miss you*. Pavel and I wanted to get a drink together last night but we ended up having a roti and then went back to his place—we thought it would be for a brief moment, but it was quarter to twelve when he walked me home. Pavel and I were there, sitting together on the fake green leather couch as he smoked; he is smoking a lot these days. Pavel and I were yelling about Helen DeWitt. Pavel asked me if I ever felt hemmed in with him or if I ever felt not free. Pavel asked me what my hesitations were and my mind went blank. Pavel blames his parents, saying they were not quite adapted to this world. Pavel bought me three small drinks, Wild Turkeys. Pavel called me earlier and sent a text message later that night. Pavel calling me, drunk. Pavel came over yesterday and as we were saying good-bye, we made out. Pavel couldn't fuck me but it was okay. Pavel didn't know that the fight was in part a game for me to get through the next few days without him. Pavel didn't seem happy when I told him the name of my project; he said, *you never told me that then*. Pavel emailed me. Pavel had an unlit cigarette in his mouth and he gave me a kiss good-bye, then he stepped into the hallway, then he stepped back into the room using the door as a kind of screen to give me another wave, and he did it a few more times, poking out from behind the door, lower and lower each time—it was funny and I laughed—finally waving good-bye to me from the floor. Pavel has given me an STD or possibly a yeast infection. Pavel has surprised me; he turned out to be a man of more substance than I thought. Pavel ignores everyone when he has a new girlfriend, and I know this because when I was his girlfriend, he ignored all of his friends. Pavel is a mess, a wreck, he cannot find his way out of this mess, and now he has even somewhat dragged me into it. Pavel is always telling me dangerous things about himself; he told me he drank twenty-four sodas the other day. Pavel is always telling me how much he loves me and asking me to never leave him and to be with him forever. Pavel is at a concert with his brother tonight, so I think he will not call because he is at the concert. Pavel is nervous about money, about never getting out of debt. Pavel is puttering in the kitchen. Pavel is so lovely and nice with the cat now, the way he talks to her. Pavel is so reasonable. Pavel is so sensitive sometimes, saying yesterday that he wanted to do my laundry, but we were out of detergent and he was running out of time, so he said he would do it when he got back. Pavel is someone around whom I can sleep and write. Pavel is staying with me this week. Pavel is still lost. Pavel is stuck. Pavel joked about his testicles being underused. Pavel jokes around a lot and makes me smile and laugh, and he makes life lighter, and yesterday he bought me that dress that made me feel beautiful, and he fucked me all day and night. Pavel just sits there and stares at his computer. Pavel kept asking me what my errands were yesterday, but I didn't tell him. Pavel left abruptly on his bike. Pavel left me a funny, strange, weird, slightly hurtful message. Pavel looked like a dog who had done something bad, begging for forgiveness. Pavel made us rice and beans, and we watched *Breaking Bad*, one episode in the TV room and one in bed, then we went to sleep. Pavel makes noises when he sleeps. Pavel pulled me back into the stairwell, and I was crying a bit and I said, *I'm weak*. Pavel said he always kind of liked how we drove everyone crazy. Pavel said he never knows what is going to set me off, that I never let things go, and that it's not compassionate not to let things go. Pavel said he was a little bit drunk. Pavel said he wouldn't ask me to marry him, but if I wanted to marry him, to let him know. Pavel said his best quality was his loving attention. Pavel said I could call him anytime. Pavel said that he had met lots of older writers in the past while, to interview them and whatnot, and that they really did have these calcified stories that they had told hundreds of times

144

before. Pavel said that he loves every part of me as much as he does every other part, and that he loves me as much as he did the first moment he saw me. Pavel said that I had to look at the wicked hand I'd been dealt. Pavel said that I have been hurting and disappointing him, blowing hot and cold, and that he has a better time alone than when he's with me. Pavel said that if I ever needed to be fucked, to be dripping, he will come over, discreetly, with his cock, and do it. Pavel said that many people have said that his smoking made them start smoking again. Pavel said that the reason we weren't living together is because we are fucking pussies. Pavel said that when he's with me he feels lonely, and then he reminds himself that we're all alone in the world anyway to avoid feeling hurt. Pavel said yesterday that he thinks once a day about putting a gun to his head and shooting himself. Pavel said, *could your cunt have a flag with the words* Property of Pavel *on it?* Pavel said, *do you want to build a life with me?* Pavel said, *how's Gil doing, anyway?* and I said, *you've never met Gil,* and Pavel said, *I know.* Pavel said, *I liked our conversation last night.* Pavel said, *I spoke to you in Russian because I'm still asleep.* Pavel said, *I want you to suck my cock,* and although I liked that he said it, I didn't want to suck his cock, and I did not. Pavel said, *there have been other girls, sure, but I always liked you.* Pavel said, *when I was younger, I used to be hurt by every little thing.* Pavel said, *your favourite guy is here*, meaning him. Pavel saw Gil caressing me, kissing the side of my face, near my hair, as I was standing by the bar. Pavel saying that I really know how to distance myself from people. Pavel should have enjoyed this early stage of our relationship, rather than tactically trying to get me to love him more by acting hurt while asking questions. Pavel smokes his cigarettes and coughs. Pavel smokes too much, but that's his choice. Pavel spent nearly the whole party in the kitchen and I drank many sidecars. Pavel thinks it was nice to have a woman really want him at a time when I was so ambivalent and uncertain; that it was nice to feel unequivocally wanted. Pavel wanted to come over, to drop by, but I told him no, then yes, then that I was torn because I wanted to write, and he said, *so write*. Pavel wanting me back, thinking he can argue me into it. Pavel was drinking the biggest beer in the place, smiling his crazy grin. Pavel was like, *look it up, almost no one responded to my birthday invitation*. Pavel was like, *this is why you don't date a writer*. Pavel was lying on one couch tonight while I was on the other, and he was reading that Edmund White book, *The Married Man*. Pavel was soft and warm and sleepy. Pavel was very eager with whoever he met, shaking their hand and widening his eyes as though he expected opportunity to come from them. Pavel woke in the middle of the night and said confusedly, *so is there no connection between the time your train leaves and the time that you were born?* Pavel wondered if I was trying to make things bad so that he would break up with me. People ate all the mozzarella sandwiches. People don't get ideas, the work comes from the soil—from a rooted place, where one is rooted, deep in the ground. People give birth to people. People need personalities to go with the books, but nobody knows who I am, so no personality can go with the books. People sure are very awkward and vulnerable when they are falling in love with you. People want to be taken away. People who looked at the weather reports knew that a storm was brewing. People who once seemed fine now have a threatening edge; I have no buffer, no man, no one protecting me. People will always need haircuts, but publishers won't always pay money for fiction. Perhaps always planning to break up is a way of gaining control over the feeling of not having control over the path of love. Perhaps he doesn't like me since I revealed myself as the fool that I am. Perhaps I am not an ethical person. Perhaps I have never really loved anybody, or let myself be loved. Perhaps I should break up with him over the phone, and perhaps that is what I will do. Perhaps I should have cried with Claire today. Perhaps I should not have called her or seen her last night, but it might not have made a difference to how I'm feeling now. Perhaps I should take a little more seriously my leaving, and not just dash off, but do it in a conscious way, think of what else I need to do and finish things before I go. Perhaps it is enough to wake up without dread and without a terrible pain in the neck. Perhaps it is not natural to be happy or to expect to be happy upon waking. Perhaps it's true what they say about the planet heating up—I mean, it's quite obviously true. Perhaps lighten my hair a bit. Perhaps one ought to get over this, just write books, think of Cormac McCarthy who just sits in his shack and writes. Perhaps related, one of the things I criticized Pavel for when we spoke on the couch about my unhappiness was that he always had an air of chaos around him, and I said it had been exhausting, and that I didn't want to be with a man who couldn't take care of himself. Perhaps that left me feeling kind of abandoned. Perhaps the body is a receptor and a reactor, not a generator, and first thing in the morning there is nothing really to stimulate it. Perhaps the book could be about what happens in a society in which people are these pure examples of extremes, but that we in fact meet in the middle, not of each other, but of ourselves, for isn't it the middle of ourselves—what is most middle—that is able to communicate with other people? Perhaps the desire to not tell stories, but forcing yourself to tell a story anyway, is what makes the book interesting. Perhaps the writer only has to attend to writing. Perhaps there will be a surge and love will return, but perhaps this really is the end. Perhaps this is the darkness of being with someone you in so many ways hate, but are so attracted to. Perhaps this is the time to try a vow of chastity. Perhaps this is the true reason I do not finish books. Perhaps this is what has been blocking me. Persevering in the good. Persona allows for privacy; authenticity allows for no privacy. Persona allows us to participate without always, at every turn, risking everything we've got. *Pheromones*, he said. Piper asked me what I liked about Pavel and I'm so glad she did, because I could say it out loud and remind myself that there are so many things, the list could have gone on and on. Piper hates him, pretty much. Piper made a masterpiece today, or something like that. Piper once laughed at me, *you think going away is being a grown-up.* Piper reminded me of what a dick Lars had been, not caring about my feelings, and leaving for Mexico a week early, even though I'd changed my ticket to come back early for him, and not telling me about his new girlfriend, and just a basic lack of respect. Piper said how nice the conversation was and I agreed. Piper today, when I told her that I was going to give up having crushes, said, *oh, you are giving up your drug!* Plane from Sydney to L.A. Played with a baby today. Polenta with delicious red sauce for lunch. Praying brings you closer to all that is good. Probably not. Psychology posits everyone as uniquely damaged, so there can be no greatness, since all great acts come out of a weakness whose lineage is long, and everything has a cause and the cause is damage, and the damage was done by another person. Put away the stuff behind the green sofa, either in the basement or in the hall. Put him off for a year, then if you still want to be with him, you can be with him after a year. Put your longing for the glamorous life into your books; you can just write things, and your books will have a better time in the minds of other people, in your absence, than you could ever have at any party.

Quiet days, not seeing people, feeling fine.

Read a lot of books. Read all day. Read *As I Lay Dying*, perhaps. Read C. S. Lewis again, *The Screwtape Letters*. Read Faulkner, who does that? Read Kierkegaard's *The Crisis and a Crisis in the Life of an Actress* twice. Read Lispector. Read philosophy. Read Ralph Ellison on the train ride home. Read some of the Weschler, need to get on that. Read Tao's new book. Read the book on Tide and whatever other business books. Read the books you brought—you have brought all the right books. Read today that Ernest Hemingway said the best state to write in is that of being in love. Reading all three of them together and the answer is simple: integrity, restraint, do not act. Reading feels like life these days. Reading his book did not help me. Reading his book helped me a lot. Reading the book about Robert Irwin while sitting on the couch, under the covers; maybe Agnes will come by and drop off my stuff in the mailbox. Reading the Kenny Shopsin book today, I just wanted four or five kids and a store and a wife. Reading the Khalil Gibran story last night about the woman who leaves her husband for her true soul husband. Really amazing, with little butterflies, and sort of a coral reef, and like little octopus tentacles and clouds and a sunset. Really I'm just spending all of my money on books. Really innocent of the world. Regretting not being in New York, a feeling I suppose I will always have. Remain aware of the dangers and in this way, surmount them. Remain with your personality in the shadows. Remember how excited you got when you thought the Spanish were going to be publishing your essays? Remember how he wasn't as tantalizing, how terrifying he was, when he was within reach? Remember how you felt yesterday after having gone shopping for underwear; that shopping is an activity, a way of spending not just money, but time. Remember how you want not to have to be special or to prove your specialness or to get your worth from any of that? Remember reading the Brecht diaries? Remember that each chapter must deliver some narrative or suspense satisfactions, so that things change from beginning to end, leading the reader forward so that they will want to finish the book. Remember that there was so much I could never have felt with him, any real intellectual or emotional depth, and how exhausting it could be, and I just want to remind my future self of this—that any fantasies about Lars have nothing to do with him, but reflect a desire to be out of whatever situation I'm in, and the inability to deal with the intensity of being with just one guy. Remember the winters of your childhood, all that snow? Remember there's nowhere else to go. Remorse, pride and modernism. Repetition makes us cynical, and something repeated loses its charm. Replace guilt with love. Replace love of God with love of the self. Reread the great short narrative books, *Elective Affinities, Dorian Gray*. Retreat correctly. Retreat probably involves taking a break from Twitter and Facebook in a serious way. Return the DVD and the cat food. Return to books as the source. Return to see the production of *Faust*. Return to Toronto and finish the book. Returning to the apartment, I missed him. Returning to Toronto, I will be on jury duty for three days. Ridiculous. Right before we parted, he picked me up and swung me around and put me back down on the steps. Right now I am cleaning the apartment for his arrival. Right now I am living on the surface of the earth. Rosa alienates everyone in deeply serious ways. Rosa asked me whether I had ever gone to a spiritualist. Rosa once said to me, *you want a boyfriend who's like Agnes*. Rosa pointed out that healthy people have healthy relationships. Rosa pointed out that I always feel anxious about every relationship, right from the start. Rosa pointed out that my shirt was always somewhat unbuttoned. Rosa said I lacked courage in not sleeping with him or seducing him. Rosa said I should have a good two weeks of discerning. Rosa said I'm taking a swim in it, rather than just, as in the past, putting my toe in it. Rosa said of our relationship problems, *instead of cowering away from the storm, just get outside in it and take off your clothes.* Rosa said that many of the relationships that are most solid and long-lasting are tumultuous at the start. Rosa said that what I was looking for was not a man, but who I was without a man. Rosa said, *just because something makes you uncomfortable, that doesn't mean you have to do it.* Rosa said, *there's enough time for everything, for difficult men, for not-difficult men, for women* . . . Rosa said, *you* are *your body, there is no distinction.* Rosa says it's a holding period. Rosa says it's no longer a holding period. Rosa sometimes wondered about not having the experience of a long-term love, and her therapist told her, *well, other people haven't had your experiences.* Rosa thinks my craving for beauty is like someone else's craving for money. Rosa told me that I was right about these literary women; that at night they suddenly cared about couture and wore glamorous dresses. Rosa told me to take care of myself first. Rosa was a bit sick or something.

Sad and scared and feeling rejected, like I'm a bad or selfish person, and that he's not speaking to me because I'm doing things wrong or because I'm bad. Sad that I'm not going to have another few weeks here to just be in my fantasies about my book. Sat in the back area where the tech people were and prepared. Saves you so many hours of pretension, affectation and lies. Saw Fiona last night and it was depressing. Saw Laurel's play: awful. Schmandkuchen is a white moussey cake with orange gelatin pieces baked into it, and Schneewittchenkuchen has cherry pieces baked into it. Schmandkuchen is white mousse with chocolate flakes on top. Schneewittchenkuchen is chocolate on top and a fork is drawn across it to create the ridges. Scrambled eggs on toast at Yaddo. Second-guessing everything. Second, he said that no one is buying fiction. See the complexity. See the souls. See what kind of story the book can accommodate, if any.

Seeing her for coffee was not so bad. Seeing her was like seeing an old friend, but maybe that's because I've watched her act in her show. Seeing him now from the outside, I don't like him as much, his variableness and lack of dependability, which always was his way—it's what he was like with his friends, he would never pick up the phone—but now it just cools my heart towards him. Seeing that house with him, I suppose there is something nice about thinking of living in it together, but I couldn't help thinking about history repeating itself, first as tragedy, second time as farce. Sell a story to Hollywood. Sell my soul and hopefully start over with a new one. Sell things on eBay that you don't need. Settle accounts, then be frugal with your money. Several weeks ago, he got his cock ring put back in. Sexiest boy in the school. She and her boyfriend are mean to each other, not tender and careful. She and him were talking at one point, leaning back on their chairs. She and I met in the hall and agreed we hadn't slept—*do you think it was the wine?* she asked, then she helped me carry my incredibly heavy suitcase down the stairs. She and I talked a bit more and she gave me her phone number and then I went back to the hotel to have a nap, and as I was falling asleep, I thought, *why not?* so I called Amandine and left a message on her phone, saying, *I know we said we might hang out when I'm next in Paris but I wonder if I can come see you tomorrow and bring my computer and maybe we can spend the day putting the book to-gether and you can translate it into French?*—and I said she'd inspired and excited me, then I woke up feeling a little embarrassed because I hadn't heard back from her, but when I checked my email, there was an email from her saying, *yes!* She appeared in the kitchen doorway and stood there as I read my story to all her friends, who were sitting in a circle around me, drinking wine, then Amandine read her translation in French, then this whole big heated discussion ensued with one of the guys saying the girl in it is too self-flagellating, and Amandine saying emphatically, *non!* She asked me if he was the man for my life. She asked me today, after seeing the flowers, *is Vig a bit in love with you?* but I didn't reply. She began counselling me, as if talking to her younger self, saying I should be asking myself of the men I encounter whether I could see myself parenting with them. She breathed, *that's genius!* She came down in her bathrobe; it was around ten o'clock at night. She came home with me and it was late and we ate ratatouille and salad and eggs. She complains and deprives herself of every indulgence, living like a mole, like a homely person, without the hope of transcendence ever. She could make her heart love all things, even what was worst, even what bad might come, even that he might never phone at all. She died suddenly of a blood clot in her leg. She felt listless without him. She felt

158

that she would dry up without a man. She had never tasted love's sweetness before. She had one kid with him, then another. She heard the door to the third floor swing open. She intended to have a sexually exploratory night with her husband, but he stayed late at work. She is a bit unfocused. She is an old woman. She is boiling water for coffee. She is cool. She is great-looking. She is nearly seventy, and it was amazing to hear her say that her life is at its best now. She is sweet and good and nice, and hopefully I can write a book that she would love. She is young. She looked flirtatiously or with a hint of a smile at the owner of the shop who, not noticing, was looking over his calculations on a single sheet of paper. She looks at men only as they relate to her life, thus reducing them. She pointed to her husband, of whom she said, *the sex was so good, we had to get married*. She pulled her overcoat on and rushed out to meet him, running down the street. She said I don't need to hold symbols so close, that it's silly. She said I needed a home, a nice apartment, and that it was the most important thing to spend money on. She said I should think of the multitude of people out there who I haven't met, who I might really want to be with, and that it could be fun, interesting, a project—a bride going in search of her groom. She said it is so much nicer to carry around a stack of paper than to carry around a computer. She said it was hard for her to write and teach and raise her son at the same time. She said it was sick that the capitalist system expects so much of people. She said Jung's conception of God was the energy that sweeps you off your plans, that comes in—the force that destroys whatever you think you are building. She said not to be the girl who pleases, but rather to make active decisions. She said of Lars, *he has the look*. She said of us, bringing her hands together, *you're mates*. She said she cried when she turned thirty-four; to her it seemed too old. She said that I have to train my mind; I don't have a bad mind, she said, but it does go in all sorts of ways, is undisciplined. She said that it's harder for older women to find men, in part because they're less pretty, but mainly because they have less sexual desire, and that if they continued to have the same degree of sexual desire as younger women, they would be nearly as desirable to men as younger women are. She said that one often stops working when things are at their closest—just before the break-through. She said that this is the realization Stephen Deda-lus had to come to. She said this was the reason for my problem. She said, *why not see if you can find someone who you have both an intellectual and a physical connection with?* She said, *you are your body, there is no distinction.* She said, *you're a writer, you have to write what you want to write.* She searched herself and produced a tiny compass. She sits on the train and is sad and feels sickened. She spoke on and on about her granddaughter; she monologues a lot, like a man. She surrounded herself with men who would adore her, making herself the only woman in her circle, the standout one, eager to please. She thinks my relationship with him is dangerous because it's not deep; it wants to prevent me from going deeper—is just interested in the moment and having a good time. She told me to wear lipstick, and yesterday it came in the mail. She took a little blue bird from underneath her dress, a little blue bird's egg, for she thought it might grow sour, not hatching, so she was trying to hatch it between her breasts. She usually gets it backwards. She was alive. She was almost dead but a little bit alive. She was being pouty and wanting me to apologize. She was giving up fashion design because it was too stupid, you had to make sixty new things every six months. She was married unhappily for fifteen years, and she called it an abusive relationship, and said that when a man insists on an apology, that is controlling, and she is happy not to be controlled, and she has never regretted leaving, has never looked back. She was talking about Martha Graham, and how Martha Graham said it takes ten years of training before the body can be free. She was the downstairs neighbour. She was the fresh air. She was the sort of person who saw lonely, solitary sadness, when all around her there was love just pouring forth, just gushing forth from every direction. She was the sort of person who saw only one apple in a tree that was just littered with apples. She will be a mother to a bird while the rest of us are drinking and crying. She will not leave him, even if she suffers by him. She wore a T-shirt that said, *I do not want your boyfriend.* Shopping is so stupid—you think about yourself in all sorts of important ways, and you're not so important in all those ways. Should I go outside and hear the bells up close? Should I try to have connections with American artists, or just think about living a simple life? Should the four of us begin having sex together? *Should we stay here or go to your room?* I asked as we walked inside, wanting to go to Tom's room, and we did. Showered and dressed up in the black cashmere sweater that Lemons sent down with Ida. Silly to be taking this trip to New York. Since I wasn't that interested in him or that attracted to him, I shouldn't have said that thing about how nice it would be to live with him in New York and be his girl-friend. Since that letter I sent him, I feel completely out of control. Since your time is now finished at the salon, you have to figure out how to make money. Smoking cigarettes again. So another woman found him, took him, got him. So embarrassing, so bad. So forget about him. So much changes all the time, I can hardly work fast enough. So the first six books are all aspects of the seventh, but what is the seventh that the first six are not? Some fall clothes, some new underwear. Some kind of organizing pleasure in writing. Some knowledge of literature. Some little cats were lying in a basket—seven little cats altogether. Some of the most important and vivid moments I have had lately are when something happens and I'm reminded on a deep level of something I encountered once in art, which the thing I'm experiencing reminds me of, so the art tells me what I'm experiencing. Some people get a lot of money. Some people get a true love. Some people like the richness of life, but I have found it to be a distraction. Some situations cannot be comfortable no matter what. Some women think their lives are not real until they are with a man. Somehow he made me feel like a barren, single girl. Somehow it makes sense that someone like him, who likes looking at himself, who spends a lot of time looking at himself, would have a back that hurts. Somehow, writing this, I am getting turned on. Something broke in me; the sky broke. Something is starting to emerge from the muck and the mud. Something more eternal, maybe. Something more than this feeling of being invisibly oppressed. Something new. Something plain-spoken about it, but okay. Sometimes good things don't have to be shared; it can be fun to have a secret for yourself, so with the person you normally tell things to, maybe don't tell them this time. Sometimes I am aware of how much work my dreams are doing, putting things into different categories. Sometimes I feel like the drug addict who thinks, *what other pleasures are there in life besides writing?* Sometimes it's even better than that: food is served, and there might be sandwiches in the middle of the table, and coffee and tea on the side table. Sometimes the sun comes in through the window. Soon it will be fall. Soon it will be July and I will be deep in my book. Sooner than I think. Speaking on the phone with him after not speaking for two days, Pavel said he was scared that I was mad at him because I hadn't replied to his last three messages. Spent last night with Gil and his friends, and we made cocktails with a pressurized can, infusing the vodka with coriander, lemongrass, tea and lime. Stability in the midst of the tumult of life. Started to feel happier about staying in Toronto. Starting all over again from the beginning. Stay away from Lars. *Stay here*, Lars told me, and it turned me on, and I stayed. Staying in Toronto is starting to feel really heavy. Still, I love it, and I will probably look back—if I do leave—and say, what a simple, pure life you had, with your friends and the cat, and your family close by, and your beautiful apartment and garden, and the projects you did with your friends, and the books you wrote, and people thinking you were smart and good—what a pure and simple life it was. Stop applying for grants; write only for the American magazines. Stop doing the column. Stop doing university gigs. Stop going onstage, travelling, all of it. Stop googling yourself. Stop reading the reviews. Stop spending money. Stop talking to anyone, everyone, about your new projects—just be quiet and think. Stop talking to people about where you are with your work, just say it's going well, for it only started going badly when you began joking about how badly it was going. Stop trying to pretend you are someone you are not. Strange that Zadie Smith and Nick Laird are in the apartment right across from us, and that I can see them and their pug from the fifteenth floor. Such a bright, shiny day. Suffice it to say that she saw only one apple on the tree, and felt sad for it, and lonely for it, while anyone could see as plain as day that the tree was just littered with apples.

Terrible day. Texting me pictures in apology. Thank God my youth is ending. That Edie Sedgwick should commit suicide. That face. That feeling I had, that pit of fear that he could not love me, is not a reason to not be with him, but a reason to *be* with him. That feels right to me, and that's the way I want to be in the world. That gives me hope for things, for everything turning out okay. That hot summer, with squares of light coming through the leaves and sparkling on the ground. That is because I got up at six this morning. That is being alive. That is how I felt when I was younger, anyway. That is how I spent my days. That is life's activity. That is the only freedom. That is the secret work no one will ever see. *That is what Hungarians do*, she said. That is what I am here to do. That is what the culture demands of female writers: to be as low as possible. That is what you can learn from writing this book. That is why I loved being with him—that love and attention and unconditional positive regard, it was just like the sun, his love, bathing me and warming me all over and making me feel so good. That is why it is important to know what one likes and what one doesn't like, what makes one happy and what does not. That made me want his cock in me. That made me want to have the internet at home. That night I lay awake for many hours, laughing with glee at how I was going to spend the rest of my life with him, and how we would live in Paris and drive his car, and I would have my new necklace, and how happy we would be, and all morning I felt like this was my life, Part 2, and I was thinking about having his children, and about writing, but not about being a writer in the way that grows more odious to me every day. That night we dressed for dinner, and there was dinner. That seems to be the way it works. That was late-winter writing. That was Sunday night. That was the first thing I wrote high. That will be the challenge, to express what is hard to express in words, because by making it concrete you lose the wisp of life, which is the essential thing. That would be a really fun project and L.A. would be the perfect place to write it, just draft it out in two long months, plan it, write it, just something quick and pulpy and fun and more complex than my own brain is. That would be a waste of my talents. That would be interesting and funny! That would be remarkable and so good. That would be so novel. That would be something special. That would pain me too much. That's all I want to know, what the human laws are. That's all that other women think about, too. That's how Grandma says you should make decisions—from what is the most important thing. The apartment has too much stuff in it. The bag, the lipstick, some clothes, the face wash. The basic problem, it seems to me, is not any of my relationships, but my own personal unhappiness. The blood which throbs through your veins. The book closed up like a scab over a wound. The book feels arid and empty to me now, like a shrivelled arm that can't raise itself to shake your hand, a withered arm and a hand. The book is beautiful and practically perfect. The book is coming along well—it's achieving beauty, symmetry, proportion, harmony and a kind of freedom. The book is difficult. The book is good. The book is not done yet, but that's okay. The book is working its way through me. The book says that everything will lead you back to writing— everything will lead you to the core of your heart. The book will come out in the future. The book you see in your head is the book it will be, and there is no better book than the book in your head, and there is no worse book than that one. The books one plans in the wake of one's book being done are too much like the book you just finished, and this will probably be the case for any books I think of here. *The Ca-*

nadian genius! Piper said, and we laughed out loud. The ceiling of her bedroom is blue. The chocolate cake I made for him, and whipped cream with raspberry sauce. The destruction of my integrity and soul. The domain of the novel really is consciousness, philosophy, story and time. The failure at living the socially sanctioned life, the life you are meant to live, results in invincibility. The fear is that it will multiply and become other fears, and I will end up a fearful person, leading a fearful little life, bolstering myself with tiny shards of evidence that I ever had any success. The first thing I do when I settle in, after checking my email and going to the hospitality suite and returning with a beer, is send an email to Lars. The first week of the new year begins. The gash on Vig's chin looked so vivid in the sun this morning. The girl floated by Hanif and giggled, *I love your writing.* The girl he was with was such an annoying and ordinary tart. The girl with the golden eye. The hairdressers were reading my story aloud yesterday, and when they came to the line about it being as simple as a car wreck, Amelia said, laughing out loud, *this one doesn't lie!* The hatred was sincere. The honey I bought for Fiona that was made by monks was confiscated at the security check—as if a sealed jar of honey made by monks! The ice in front of the front door this winter is so thick, like an ice floe, that I have to hold on to the mailbox every time I come in through the door. The idea of a relationship makes me sick. The idea of it fills me with loathing, a boredom so profound I cannot stand to think of it. The idea of raising a child and having a family. The idea of this terrified me profoundly. The idea that I am not circumscribed or defined by my work. The image my mother had for me was: be a scientist, don't go to clown school, don't have sex before marriage, work hard, get married, have children, be happy. The insanity started around then, and I can't recall much of it, except that I woke and felt it was the scariest dream I'd ever had because it said my brain was crazy, and I kept shouting and was hysterical and screaming and felt insane. The kid told me he'd bought three copies of my book to give to his friends. The kids invited me to a peanuts party. The kiss of death. The life you have chosen. The little boy wouldn't let anyone touch his toys and dumped his plate upside down on the table, staining the tablecloth with ketchup. The man on the airplane said that you can cause problems for yourself if you are always trying to find out the reason why. The man on the streetcar said he sometimes wondered if there weren't enough brains distributed at the beginning of the world. The memory of when your body was entirely yours. The modernist ethic which taught that unhappiness must be the centre of an artist's life. The more I enjoy music, the more I want sex. The most delicious-smelling man. *The new apartment will put an end to this bad time*, Rosa said, but it hasn't been an altogether bad time. The next day Gil came over and I gave him a haircut, and he was rubbing himself into me. The next day I decided that I would move with him to New York, but by then it was too late, he had already soured on me. The next day we made a breakfast of eggs and toast, then we went to a music store nearby. The next day we slept all morning. The one thing I can say was that I had been sick and unhappy and lonely, and I called him on the phone and said we should get married. The only reason I would not be a good writer in Toronto is because of this cloud of doubt which takes up my entire mind. The only thing that clutters me truly is email and seeing people too much, and I can control all of that. The other day, the morning I got home from Montreal, when I so much had to work, Pavel tied me up, but I didn't really want to be tied up, I wanted to work. The other thing I realized was that I always thought I had to love other people the way a person loves a child, but then I looked at the people around me—my friends—and I realized they were adults. The other thing I'm realizing is how easy it is to end something; that the universe allows things to end. The pain and turmoil of listening to her talk about Lemons. The part of the brain that sees patterns is less intelligent than the part that sees probabilities. The part that sees patterns compares this time to the week I left for Spain. The part that sees probabilities notices how rare Lars is. The passage of time is the funniest thing. The perfect haircut and clothes, the perfect skin, the perfect brightness in the eyes, the perfect posture, the perfect manners, the perfect way of relating to people you have a heavy emotional charge with. The point is not to attach to the details of your life. The point is to let go. The present emphasizes all other presents resembling this present. The problem of eternity. The problem was that the banging and hammering were keeping me up—and Ellis and his girlfriend said the same thing, that they'd been woken up at six, and she had looked at the ceiling and said, *fuck.* The question for me since New York has been, does he love me and want to be my boyfriend? The question, Rosa said, is, *does he want to spend the rest of his life with you?* The questions for marriage are like, *do I want my brother to have to talk to him?* The rabbi said, *imagine how people in Auschwitz did it, how they felt—in the same cold, but with only a sheath on, wooden shoes, no food and no sleep*, so everyone continued digging her grave but without any more complaining. The rain is coming down, and now there's sun and a rainbow. The rest is a romantic story. The salon is a stage. The same in a poem as in a face. The same is true in every heart on earth. The secret pleasures and gifts of adulthood are mostly hidden from the young. The sex is something you can trust. The shirt was up behind the pillow. The simple rearranging of pastries at a bakery. The smell of his cum was beautiful, was everywhere, and his saliva tasted so sweet. The story of Narcissus, who falls in love with his own image and is caught up in its spell—and what, does he kill himself? The streetcar took a detour. The streetlights are on because it's night. The struggle through it all was how to make writing primary over love, when love insisted on its primacy. The task now is to speak truthfully. The taste of lemon cake on Pavel's lips. The thing I like most to feel is what I felt when I was seventeen, reading. The thing is to send the book out on Friday, whether or not it is done. The thing to think about is how to have characters acting as other characters, playing the role of the characters they are playing. The trees are rustling. The true measure of things. The Tuscan hillside is beautiful, and the olive groves with their silvery leaves are so beautiful. The value of adventure is low right now, and the value of starting the novel is high. The whole time, the whole of my twenties, I had the sense that I was doing the wrong thing, but I couldn't have told you what the right thing was, except that possibly it was the opposite of whatever I was doing. The work went really well today, and I had the feeling that it had to be the best book written in the last few years, but as I write this down, I think, what do I know of books being written in the last few years? The world doesn't need anything from me. The world doesn't see me, no one is bothering to judge. The world has its place for all of us. The world is great, not mediocre, and I am a part of it. The world moves along well enough without my art. The young man with the umbrella who biked from Munich. Then back to New York this fall. Then back to Toronto to see what's what. Then back to your book for the rest of the spring. Then cleaning the house. Then cooking dinner. Then Gil came over and we fucked. Then Hanif felt better, and was finally able, in his fifties, to have a deep and truly loving relationship with a woman, without feeling that he was betraying his mother by doing so. Then he came over, and we had the most loving day ever between us, and wonderful sex all day and night, and before going to sleep Vig asked me to cuddle him from behind, and I did, then an hour later he turned around and said, *clothes off, please*, and I took mine off and he did, too, and we made out really slowly and hot, then I gave him a blow job and then I lay in his arms for a long time. Then he got in the bath with me, and this is the night when he was going down on me for so long, and I was thinking about Lars. Then he kind of took my head in his hands and pushed me down onto my back, and we started fooling around some more. Then he left for work and I slept, and napping I had a dream. Then he realized the time and had to go to work. Then he reassured me that though he doesn't drink or do drugs, he does have other vices. Then he said, *what is your name?* and his eyes flickered across the alley, paved in stones. Then he spat on me. Then he went to get a cigarette and I could smell him smoking. Then he went to get his bike and I walked through the neighbourhood and started to miss him, and it made me happy that I could stay with him, even though things were bad; that the difficulties didn't mean I had to leave. Then he wrote to apologize and I wrote back that I couldn't live like this, and he had to see someone about his anger problems. Then he yelled at me some more. Then her grandmother started talking—she was single, and she was talking about some drama in a recently past relationship, clearly obsessed with it above all else, and I thought about how distasteful it was to see an old woman obsessing about her romantic relationships—and I saw it was possible; that a woman really could do that her whole entire life, and I realized how important it was to stop. Then I asked him what he thought the worst quality was for a person to possess, and he said, *what do* you *think it is?* and I said my first thought: *being an intellectual.* Then I asked the man on the streetcar why he thought people looked at the world the wrong way, and he said, *I don't know, maybe they have a game in their head?* Then I ate pastrami sandwiches with Ellis, and we had onion rings and I ordered a pickle, then we had tea and coffee and walked down to St. Mark's for the Japanese ballet, and after the show I felt like I wanted the grace of the woman dancer with the parasol, and I felt that the beauty of her movements came from a purity of heart, and that from purity of heart could spring purity of movement. Then I felt more confident and reentered the party. Then I realized I would never stop writing. Then I realized it's because it feels so good to work. Then I saw that having dignity meant thinking, using my reason, not just my instincts and emotions. Then I spoke with a woman whose two daughters live in New York because she encouraged them to go to Columbia, where one of them met her husband in the Jewish residence. Then I started to cry. Then I started to think of people I did love, and I said unequivocally that I loved my brother. Then I thought, *I will have sex with just one more person the rest of my life*. Then I told myself, *it's okay to feel that*, and then the feeling was gone. Then I went down to the water and prayed. Then I went home in a cab, and I felt that this travelling and touring were not good for me, because it put me around people who were admiring of me, which felt corrupting or bad. Then I went out into the streets and looked in the stores. Then I went to have lunch with his mother to get advice about my life, and she compared my relationship to the one with her ex-husband, which she said was abusive, and I talked about how bad I felt all the time, and about how he always wanted me to apologize, and I decided to break up with him soon. Then I went to the Price Chopper to get us food for dinner, and he gave me a cute little list to take with me. Then I went upstairs once more and came back down again, too shy to ask Ellis to dinner, but the second time, I did. Then I went with Claire to that Vitello Fresh place and we had lunch, and she opened up in a normal and human way, and I felt like we could be friends, and that we had things in common in a confidential and womanly way; that is, I felt that we could talk as women, and I understood her to be an artist, and the way that she is one. Then I will find another man and will leave him. Then I will rue leaving him, even though it will not have been the wrong thing to do. Then I woke up in the middle of the night and my body felt better than it ever had, just sparkling, and my muscles felt so alive. Then in London, Adam Thirlwell and I watched *Nymphomaniac* two days in a row, and I accidentally ended up sending an email to Lars von Trier from his phone. Then in the bar for the second time, Lemons was saying that he thought he would have a life in which he was always romantically troubled, and I said I did think he had the capacity to fall in love in that complete and total way that he was always hoping to. Then in the late hours, it kind of switched, and I saw that his feelings were his, and that I didn't have to have them, too, and that the walls of the relationship didn't have to move one bit because of his bad feelings, and that it's all right and natural for a person to feel upset. Then in the shower I felt very desirous, and sad that we didn't have sex as much as I wanted, but then I realized that whenever, in the past, I had been feeling desirous, it wasn't long before we did have sex, so I told myself I should relax about it, so I did, then he, without any prompting from me—though I came to bed naked—went down on me, and later he asked me for a blow job. Then it happened all of a sudden—like a flash across the dark sky, lighting up the entire landscape for just a single moment. Then it was raining, and I put on my hat and scarf and walked in the rain to Vig's place. Then my mind freed itself of men and spun out this long, long movie which was incredibly abstract and brilliant, and it was my mind telling me what I would be capable of if I didn't think about men all the time. Then no email from him at all. Then once I had the bread and cheese and was standing in the street, it really did look like a little French town, and it was overcast and unfamiliar, and I suddenly felt happy. Then seeing Claire on Instagram with Barack Obama, and that she is going to be on *SNL*, I became so jealous I couldn't stand it. Then someone began handing out plastic flutes, and the champagne was poured into glasses, and photographs were taken, and all the photographers were rushing about, huddling people close together. Then something happened between me and the attractive boy on the streetcar—a smile. Then swallow down his cum while he lies on the bed, rocking you back and forth with both his hands. Then taking a walk. Then telephoning family. Then the very next day I saw Pavel in the swimming pool and couldn't stop laughing, finding myself still so attracted to him, and still liking him so much. Then today I gave a copy of the new draft to Lemons. Then today I was thinking about how I don't need to justify everything, and that this is the cause of so much of my misery, this constant monologue in my head, as though I have to account for the way I am, my every action, my entire existence. Then we lay on the couch and watched *Requiem for a Dream*. Then we stared at each other for a long time. Then we talked in Lemons's kitchen about his being in love with Ida. Then we text-messaged for a bit and he was trying to be apologetic, but he only got meaner. Then we touched each other, and he pulled and pushed on the belt loops of my jeans, while I lay on my stomach, eyes closed, head turned away, as he kissed my waist and hip. Then we went back to Elif's apartment and ordered food, then I packed and we smoked on her balcony, and we decided not to write about our trip right then because we both were tired, and we went to bed but neither of us slept, we both kept getting up to go to the washroom, and several times I smoked on her balcony. Then we were offered champagne and I turned it down, for I am sick of champagne. Then when we were halfway to the Hôtel de Ville, he pulled his invitation to the embassy out of his bag and I realized I had forgotten mine, or rather I didn't even know we needed it, so I ran back to the hotel. There are an infinite number of ways of going wrong. There are just so many millions of factors, it's amazing anyone charts a path through life. There is a great difference between being sorrowful because you see that the world is without justice, and because you see the world and your place in it as being unjust. There is a great unity in a person, and all things work together, and you can't take out the parts that you don't like or don't understand or which feel inconvenient to you. There is a little space inside me that can sometimes become occluded, but sometimes I can feel it as an actual oasis of clarity. There is no answer, no way out of life, no avoiding what life has in store for you. There is no ideal love. There is no set future that one tumbles towards, helplessly, as if down a hill. There is nothing I have done wrong, though it gave me a pang to see that smile on his face when I asked whether they were going to have children, and he said, *presumably*. There is nothing more to say to him, nothing. There is nothing so grand about being alone, I don't see what's so great about it. There is so much I'm going to miss about him. There is so much inside me now, and so much work to be done. There is so much to think about and do. There is something grotesque about having been given so much yet to spend all your time drinking—yet he was saying that it's also grotesque to think you were put on this earth to deliver an answer. There is something nice about my face, I think. There is the sweet smell of life growing everywhere. There is the sound of birds and a lawn mower. There must be other ways to write a diary than all this minutiae; I don't want another night at home with all my thoughts. There was a beach, the most deserted and nicest beach in all of Europe. There was a big confusion in my head about whether to get him the brass bear, the brass elephant, the walking stick, or none. There was a kind of daybed in Tom's study and we sat on it, up against the cushions, and drank the vodka and talked. There was a park we lay around in and later it started to rain. There was a point in the night when we had to get on the boat to take us back to the mainland. There was emailing in the afternoon in tents. There was salt on my lips, and when I licked them, they tasted salty. There was some hostility somewhere. There you are on the internet. These are the nicest times. These ten years of wandering might, one day in the future, seem to have been necessary. These tight deadlines I am giving myself are sapping me of the joy of writing. They all think they are failures; all the good ones know the extent to which they have failed. They are actual people, modelling as characters. They are the king and queen of my world. They bore you and make you feel restless. They change their domain, instead of their domain changing them. They figure out their problems on their own, not going to their friends. They had a beautiful loft, and hanging out the window at one point, smoking a cigarette, I turned and asked them when they'd first met. They had been together only six months. They have been married twenty years. They kind of laughed at me when I thought it was caviar. They need each other to function. They never have any new stories. They never seem much in doubt or to feel ashamed. They probably had sex on this couch. They stay within their economic and class strata, yes. They want to know that after suffering comes salvation, and that salvation will come in the form of fame. They were just down the road. They were living in the moment. They were very confident, hiding away any signs of loss or distress. They would like us to keep our outfits nice, so when we take them out to dinner, we don't look like ruffians. They're empty inside. Things are dying and falling off, like when the man in *The Fly* changes into a fly. Things are getting softer and calmer with him. Things are hard and should be expected to sometimes be hard. Things became uncomfortable when he said I had used him. Things have been incredibly hard with Vig, and last night he said he couldn't stay in the relationship if it was going to continue to be like this. Things I thought about while lying under the stars. Things pass quickly into the past. Things were good with us today, really sweet.

Things with him are going well. Things with him were getting better, but then during sex last night it was the same old problem—I just don't get into it with him. Think about him less, and think about God and the millions of other people more. Think about Leibniz. Think of the qualities you needed to make the book turn out: faith, patience, perseverance. Thinking about him all the time and all the negative things he might be thinking of me, like why he doesn't respond to my emails or calls, and how, when he doesn't, I imagine he is feeling contempt for me for being weak, or weak for expressing vulnerability, and to imagine I am being demanding or exhausting—this lowers my self-esteem, to imagine this is his feeling about me, whether or not it is true. Thinking about moving to Berlin, I began to feel a deep pit of loneliness, meaningless, and despair. Thinking about lovers is a form of vanity, another form of thinking about oneself. Thinking about men is a default; what would you rather think about? Thinking about the world and just being in it often casts a greyish hue. Thinking about Vig and how he is giving himself to me. Thinking has been an armour against living, against the world, myself, my instincts, the moment, God, and other people. Thinking last night in bed about how much nicer it is to commit to something—someone, an action, reading a book, following something through to the end. Thinking that if there ever comes a time when I really want to write one great story, it would be useful to develop the parts of my brain that I think the best writers have, and which they must have, given the evidence of their books. Thinking yesterday that it is the days when I don't want to write, when my feelings are such that I can't possibly write, and when my inclination is certainly not to write—that then is especially when I should write. This belief that we almost have some moral duty to pamper ourselves, to understand and know ourselves, and that self-knowledge of this kind will save our souls, when actually it is a kind of blindfold. This bourgeois life was always my destiny. This coddling of the self, this aiming for self-hood, and all the great gifts of self-actualization. This craft is really just whining. This desire to categorize monopolizes my time and my desire to write. This desire to order and organize, to make an architecture and understand. This desire to transcend, to break the rules of time and space. This excited me as I rode my bike. This had never occurred to me! This had the opposite effect on me, and I thought it was greedy of Pavel to be wanting so much of my love, when I was giving him all he had the right to expect, and which he should have enjoyed at this early stage of our relationship, rather than tactically trying to get me to love him more by acting hurt while asking me questions. This is insane to me. This is just my heart. This is not helpful, writing like this.

This is not something that is easily resolved. This is not the place I want to create from anymore. This is not what I have a brain for. This is one of those emotionally intense periods when I write little because things are too changing. This is part of a continuation of a long series of things, and I really feel, waking up in the middle of the night like this, my mind talking to itself in such a repetitive and meaningless way, that I would simply have too much to think about if I was with a man. This is perhaps why everything burns up, or why I burn everything up. This is probably because this morning I was lying in bed, feeling such a rage towards him, feeling like men always want to steal my soul and take things from me and put me in a situation, and as I was telling myself this, I was imagining hitting and punching him. This is some kind of quiet crisis carrying itself out inside me, that I am not even fully participating in. This is the first day of using the new computer. This is the first day of the year. This is the first page, this is the beginning, and all the other pages can come after. This is the last time I publish with them. This is the least interesting thing I could be writing right now, when so much happens in my life that would be very interesting to record, but I just never have the energy. This is what I was praising Vig for when I told him that he had the mind of a novelist, for he is always categorizing and classifying people. This is what I was thinking about as I was wandering through the castle grounds, when the light was all pastel and soft, and several old people were walking by. This is what makes living increasingly difficult—that one has other times to compare with the present. This is when he and I started to like or trust each other again, since we both were laughing. This may have been the night that we talked all night, or it could have been the next night. This morning I saw that I had bruised my thigh but I wasn't sure how. This morning over a breakfast that Pavel made, he asked me if I had a good time talking to Gil, because it sure looked like I did. This morning, walking to get coffee alone, I felt good because I realized that I was strong within and could act morally. This next book has to be about people interacting, doesn't it? This was the show in the anarchist place, when I got high and wrote the email to everyone. This was the show in the field. This was the show where they laid out cigarettes for us and matches, but my pack got lost or stolen while I was onstage; I should have left them in the van. This was the weekend that Vish hog-tied me, fucked me up the ass for the first time, and said, *hey bitch, did I ask for your opinion?* when I was saying *no no,* when he was trying to go deeper into me, but then when he was really fucking me, it felt amazing. This was upsetting to me and I accused him of having deeper feelings for the people in

Moscow than he did for me, and he got offended that I would say that, and I ended up yelling at him and calling him an asshole and walking away with a medium-happy feeling in me, and he pointed his finger at me, at my retreating head, like a gun. This will come up in every relationship. This will lead to a life of insanity. Though I am in debt now, for the first time ever. Though I am uneasy to be living so luxuriously, anyway. Though it did occur to me in line at the airport today that the chroniclers are at the top of the heap. Though lying in bed with him last night, I had a sense of how long life is, and how young I am relative to how much there is to go. Three years since breaking up with him. Throw out as much as possible. Throw out more books. Time is going by. To appease which angry gods? To assert that life is happening. To be a grand woman. To be able to look everyone in the eye on his wedding day and truly host the party because he feels no shame—just absolute certainty about having chosen the right wife—this was Lemons's greatest dream. To be anchored to the world differently. To be calm in the face of it. To be in a calm place, and not distract myself to such an extent that I no longer know what a calm place is. To be neither beautiful nor famous nor eccentric. To be the champion? To be the one? To beware of mirages of any sort. To carry on the anger is to carry on the drama and bind myself to him still. To clean out the fridge and the cupboards. To cultivate real self-control, a real patience with the world, and a philosophical acceptance of things as they are, rather than striving to make things as I would have them be—surely different writing would come out of that than this turbulence and confusion. To develop a philosophy of living. To every day go through a catalogue of the people in my life to make sure I've attended to the care of each. To fashion one's life. To get groceries. To get the man you need, which will fortify your life and your soul and your heart. To give up on the idea of children, which was becoming the next thing to race to. To have his child and soon. To have this obligation to make things? To live aloneish. To live to think about the world and write it. To make a decision and follow through. To make at least $40,000 a year. To move slowly, rather than expecting miracles overnight—just a steady, plodding movement in a new direction. To not abbreviate. To not call my friends. To not pick up and check my phone. To not write him when I want attention as a distraction from pain. To notice how things go back and forth. To put an end to that period, the book must be published. To say something in the world. To say this and not that. To stay in one place long enough to watch something grow, for if you know something about how one thing evolves, maybe you can extrapolate and know how everything does. To talk to the mountain? To think of how I threw myself at him in that email! To think we would have found happiness together!—that seems unlikely any way you look at it. To try to keep my feet on the ground. To wash the dishes. To withdraw projection. To write one thing that is honest instead of a pack of lies well said. To write the book about being a loser. To write this book again. To write with the thoroughness of my whole being for the rest of my life. Today I shampooed the hair of a man named David who is the conductor of the orchestra at the National Ballet. Today I watched six episodes of *Millionaire Matchmaker*. Today I went to the T-shirt store across the street to see if I could play with their cat. Today I wore my hair pulled back, my white stockings and my low heels with the cut-outs at the sides, and my short black dress from H&M, and my flight-attendant-looking jacket. Today is Lemons's wedding. Today is Thursday. Today is Tuesday. Tonight he said that pain was not punishment, and I cried in bed with him, although I'm not sure he knew it; I was silent, his arm was around me, my head was turned to the wall, all the lights were off in his room and tears were coming down my face. Too bad he didn't show up. Took a walk through the mental health centre. Toronto felt to me yesterday like putting on soft pajamas. Toronto may well be a coastal city one day. Toronto means nothing to me anymore. Toronto, Toronto, Toronto, fine. Turned off phone. Turned thirty. Two minutes into the conversation, Lemons laughed and brightly said, *I thought you were calling to tell me you were engaged!* Two soups sitting in the fridge, neither of which I could eat.

Unloved. Unstable because of him. Upon reading all of this, my anxiety instantly vanished and I shut down the computer and ran to bed, happy and excited—thrilled, really. Upset that this is now the second time the internet is not working. Use reason to make decisions, rather than emotion which has tricked me in the past. Use whatever techniques you want and remember what you first knew: that it doesn't matter what the book is about.

Vig and I have been watching *The Wire*. Vig and I kissed several times. Vig and I were talking about having dinner together tonight. Vig and I were talking on the phone when he said that he wanted to skip a day of talking. Vig called after I texted and he could tell I was upset, and he said his apologies, but not in a simpering way, just showing that he understood why I was upset; then I said I didn't feel like talking and could we get off the phone. Vig came calmly, smiling. Vig came out of the bathroom. Vig feeds the rabbits, and I feel like a rabbit, too. Vig feeds the squirrels and puts out peanut butter sandwiches for them. Vig felt I was not giving him what he needed, asked for, the space he needs to decompress, be by himself, without me trying to connect with him. Vig got out of bed and now he's sitting on the purple couch, putting on his shoes. Vig had me take off my clothes last night to show him my body while he was at work and I was in my hotel in the Marais, and I felt myself blushing for hours after. Vig is a little resentful of his twenties, of the women and relationships which took up so much of his time. Vig is intelligent and interesting and funny. Vig is intelligent, loving and kind. Vig is not a layabout with no money. Vig is very good at logic. Vig is very good at seeing things. Vig just came in and said I had to be careful these next couple of days because he took the pin out of my table and now the leg is not attached to the table; he's going to the hardware store to get something to repair it with. Vig likes to get up, not lie around all day. Vig looks like someone who will keep contributing to the world, not like someone who has stopped, but like someone who is just starting. Vig makes a point of never telling a story in the same way, always making it a little bit different in the details or the emphasis. Vig met and had a long conversation with an old girlfriend. Vig never takes responsibility for what happens when we fight, it's always entirely my fault. Vig never wants to talk. Vig obligingly talked about it with me for a while, then abruptly changed the subject. Vig often says, *I don't want to talk about this now*, in his domineering way. Vig pointed out yesterday that the subjects that bring me stress are often the ones I bring up myself—his old girlfriends, us moving in together. Vig said he didn't think women were that way, wanting to sleep with a man after they'd already decided they didn't like him. Vig said he knew that I had never loved a man like him before, but we didn't get very far into discussing what sort of man he was before we went back to reading our Kindles. Vig said he was going to leave me there for two hours as he went to get a dildo, and I begged him not to leave, and he said he was going to, and I sobbed and sobbed. Vig told me not to act like a child.

W alk more and be outside more. Walking home from the party, I was upset, thinking Agnes had it all because she had a husband, and now she could have a kid, while I had nothing. Walking to the bar where I was going to think about my future, it seemed like it would be good to have the novel in shape by February. Walking to the Price Chopper yesterday, he asked me if we had ever before walked together when there was snow on the ground. Walking up the street last night, I saw myself as stepping off a spinning wheel. Walking was also falling. Walking with him in the bookstore, we were talking and looking at books, and I spotted the literary fiction section, and it suddenly seemed like the smallest thing in the world, not at all this huge thing, or the most important thing in the world, but like some precious cabal with a lot of self-importance.

Wandering and wandering. Wandering in Toronto. Wandering just this little patch of earth. Wanting to be open to whatever the future might bring. Wanting to be protected. Wanting to control something that cannot be controlled. Wanting to cry. Was he sexist? Was I sixteen? Was it only Tuesday when we had steak tartare at Le Poisson Rouge and Pavel cried, and I cried, too? Was it too late to be loving? Was it worth it to be doubtful, to be so paralyzed with doubt? We agreed that he was smart, maybe the smartest person we knew. We all do different things well, and pick up on and admire most in others the qualities we do not have in ourselves. We all have our vanity. We are all connected. We are always loyal to the wrong people. *We are just a couple of adults having a good time*, he said. We are sitting here in bed, and he is writing a letter, but even if he didn't have a letter to write, the morning wouldn't have moved towards sex. We are unique little planets. We ate a lot of nice food—green beans and mussels and potato kugel and red cabbage, and neither of us mentioned wine, we just drank water. We ate our shrimp risotto on the couch, then he quietly and carefully brought up the idea that we should go to couples therapy together. We ate the first of many sandwiches. We both feel insecure. We can only look out at the world. We can understand ourselves by understanding a cup, a cloud, a car, a pot, a piece of seaweed. We can't look at humans directly because it's too hard. We can't look at ourselves. We can't see where our cruelty or selfishness comes from. We didn't even discuss it, it was just understood. We didn't have sex for weeks because we didn't feel intimate or sexual, and we were fighting, and sex is not part of our fighting. We don't even notice the things about ourselves that are noticeable to others, like that I can type without looking at the keys. We don't have a reigning morality. We don't have a unified religion or philosophy. We don't know what to be afraid of. We don't satisfy each other, and we have barely slept together these past nine months. We drank long into the night. We drank white wine and he sat on a chair by the window and read my novel, which I'd printed out, and I fell asleep on the bed. We gossiped about Lemons, and Ellis told me that he'd kissed Ida, and I said, *what do you like about her?* and he said, *she's pleasant*, and he kept using that word, *pleasant*, but he said he'd only been going for her lips in the way you kiss your friend's girlfriend on the mouth, which I found strange. We got nachos, and Lemons was grave, and this was because of Ida wanting to leave him, and I could feel coming off his skin the vapours of the confusion and whirl one is in after something like that happens. We got up and lay in the brittle grass, but it felt so bad that we finally walked on and left the park, running into the dancer and her husband in the road. We had a bit of a fight about Ida, and from that point on I was deeply exhausted and I still haven't recovered. We had a bit of a fight about my old bed, which we finally threw away. We had a bubble bath, then Vig went down on me and we fucked. We had a conversation last night in which I said it's not a novel but a book, and that I like books more than I like novels. We had a little relationship that ended ambiguously. We had a wonderful, funny time. We had ice cream. We hailed a cab in the street and hugged and kissed goodbye. We have been holding things together just barely, and now our grip has loosened. We have different needs, I guess. We have had such a pleasant night; he's been playing video games while I have been working and writing. We have lost the art of privacy, of keeping things to ourselves, hidden behind a persona. We have returned to the early days of self-help, when self-help books were character sketches of the world's greatest men. We have something nice between us already. We have to find new subjects. We have to keep ourselves tidy. We held hands the whole way home. We hung around a long time. We joked about what if there really was a heaven, then he would be married to Mom for eternity. We laughed and laughed. We lay down on the grass in the park and slept. We lay in bed all morning, until two p.m. on Friday, which was the last day of the year. We left and went to a bar and talked, then we went to meet Adam's wife at another bar, but it was too loud and so we returned to the original bar where I ate scampi chips—or crisps or whatever they're called—then went back to their place and called an Addison cab. We listened to the concert in the car. We live, perhaps for the first time in history, in an age in which people can fuck up their lives in a hundred different ways without social disapproval, and this freedom can feel impinged upon by a moral lesson about living, so no one wants to read those stories, we just want to make our mistakes. We looked in some shops, then we looked in some more shops, then I agonizingly bought the elephant made of bronze and wood. We loved each other and the difficulty was there. We met a nice cat. We played a game with words in a hat. We returned to the Intersteer, where we had first started drinking, then we went to a bar called The Local and sat in the window and continued to talk, and I explained to him that the gelato place across the street was where I had first been waiting for him because I had thought the Intersteer had changed into the gelato place. We said good-bye and I went upstairs, sure of him and everything. We saw each other and we couldn't stop smiling, so overwhelmed with glee and possibility. We smiled at each other, me from in the street, and he from a window in his house. We spoke as though it was the last time we would ever speak, and I was in tears. We started getting bitten by the mosquitoes, so we decided to go inside. We stood by the doorway, drinking cherry brandy from a sour cream container, then we saw the two of them walking by, Lars with an L markered on his cheek, under his eye, like a teardrop. We talked a bit and reminisced about life, and I told Piper of how I had met Vig, and she laughed and said she took the story a different way: that Vig always found people to admire him. We talked for several hours. We took a room in the hotel and lay on the bed, too tired to walk or move or do anything. We turned into particles and fell on the beach as particles, sparkling. We walked through the rain to the gallery. We walked towards West House, in the direction of the pool, as we drank from the blue goblet. We walked up and down the hills yesterday on our way to the village, and it was sunset, and the clouds were red and pink, and the village in the distance was reddish with earth. We went to bed without saying good night, and this morning I still feel hardened inside, and I woke up thinking that the best thing would be to never be with another man ever. We were in a car together and the streets were snowy and icy. We were living in a world that had very dark skies. We were on an interminable streetcar ride, but it was also a special one; condensation was covering the windows, and it felt like there was no outside, and the light inside was artificial and the air was damp but cozy. We were reading the newspaper together. We were sitting around a table, and Ida was reading to us a list of things she could eat: lemons and meringue. We were talking about

Jung, and how he was saying that ritual is the way the conscious mind communicates with the unconscious mind, so if you want to kill someone, it's enough to enact that gesture with something that is not the person—to imbue another object with the properties of the person you want to kill—and if the emotion is there, it will be to the unconscious mind as if you had really done it. We were talking about love, and he admitted that he felt in love with me at moments, definitely, and he said that he told himself not infrequently that he loved me or was in love with me. Well, that's very convenient! What a boring life, to always be rehashing the same old things. What a charlatan, who skims the surface of everything—no direction, no will, a faker, a flake, a know-nothing. What a hot sun! What a load of rubbish all this writing is. What a stupid thing to do. What a terrible week it's been. What am I going to do? What beauty could be made from this randomness? What bullshit this is. What can a person accomplish in fiction without a memory? What can you learn from the other arts that you cannot learn from this one? What century am I living in that I have to pay my debts to modernism? What did Beckett know? What do actors know? What do I have to be so afraid of? What do I want to do this year? What do most people do in a year? What do the birds do? What do you want to do more than anything else in the world? What does it all add up to? What does it mean to love writing? What happened all summer long? What happened on Saturday? What happened was that I arrived, and he was at the bar, and he looked different from how I'd remembered him looking; after a year of emailing I had forgotten, and was startled and sort of horrified by this wild-haired and frantic creature, hysterical and loopy and older, and I think I said something to express my disappointment, something along the lines of, how while all along *he* knew what *I* looked like, he had not sent me any pictures of himself—and there I was, stranded with him in New York, and I would have to sleep with him in his bed for a week. What have I done? What I have done is what I have always done. What is this cycle all about? What the hell did I think the next book would be about? What will be next? What will the story be? What will you do with all of your time? What you call abbreviation is actually impatience. What you hate most in life are the interruptions and the surprises, that is, life itself. *What's new with you?* Claire asked, when I very well just told her in an email! Whatever looks like an avenue of life cut off turns into a terror inside me. Whatever. When bad things happen, don't dwell on them. When he calls, what will I do? When I live according to ethics, I don't feel I'm living honestly. When I looked at the wall, I saw a second moth like the first, its white wings soft and laced in dust. When I remind myself that I am inferior to nobody, my attachment to him loosens. When I returned from the store, he was just coming out of the shower. When I returned to my email, there was a long message from Lemons. When I think of another thirty years of writing, it seems impossible to explain. When I thought that I didn't enjoy sex because it was emotional, now I think I enjoy it because *it is* emotional. When I told Rosa that I used not to have feelings, but now I have them all the time, she said maybe I was too weak to have feelings before. When I was talking about geniuses on the couch, Lars said, *they just add objects to the world.* When I was with him, he admitted that he was usually half-drunk when he emailed me. When I went to peek out at the city I hadn't yet had a chance to see, pulling aside the heavy hotel drapes, the sky was already yellow and the sun was low on the horizon, wavering a few inches above it, shining its bright halo a direct signal into my mind, and I thought, *I will never sleep again.* When I woke up, I decided to get an external hard drive. When I woke up, I did not feel relief, because things are still hard. When I woke up, I felt heavy and sad. When I woke up, I remembered what happened. When I woke up, it was the middle of the night. When it comes down to it, in the pit of me, I prefer being alone and imagining things in isolation rather than actually dealing with the world, though maybe everyone is also that way. When Pavel left, we kissed each other on the cheek and collarbone, then

I held on to his hand and kissed it. When she asked me why I didn't feel things when I was younger, I said it's because I lived in a dream; I had a sense of unreality about everything. When she said that she thought it was going to be a good year, I felt she was touching my year with her magic. When we arrived at the American embassy, I found my way into the room in which they were serving, of course, more champagne, and a young man approached me and said, *so what's this project all about?*—he worked at the embassy and was very much a young Washington type, telling me all about his opinions when I hadn't even asked, and all of his opinions were expressed clearly and simply and in ordinary sentences. When we did fuck, it was incredible. When we got up after a long night of drinking, we had chocolate, madeleines, oranges, scotch and tea. When we touched each other, there was nothing. When will I ever change? When you are fifty-five, sixty, or sixty-five. When you are jealous of other people, you forget there is a place in the world for you, that you occupy a real and legitimate place. When you break up with someone, you feel you must have had such incredible powers of self-deception to have gone out with them at all. When you don't spend money, it adds energy to your art. When you look through your bookshelf on grey-soul days, on soul-overcast days, that's the book that you choose. Where is the gold coin he gave me, that lovely man? While chopping all the firewood. White ceilings with beautiful chandeliers hanging down, and not too many crystals. White glare of publicity. Who cares? Who cares? Who do you know at *The New Yorker*? Who else? Who wants to live a long time? Whose life is without its messes? Why can't I just be happy and organize my life as I would like it to be, as I most want to live it? Why do I feel like I'm playing around? Why do I look for symbols? Why do women go mad? Why does one bra clasp in the front and the other in the back? Why don't I go somewhere warm, where there is the ocean and I can swim every day? Why is all this coming out now? Why is this drama necessary? Why not just accept things? Why not let the worst occur? Why shouldn't I have him, if he's the one that I want? Why shouldn't this happiness be mine? Why work? Why write? Will I always write? Will I have nothing inside me anymore, one day? With darkness comes the sunset, and with the sunset comes the rain. Woke up because I was drunk. Worked on the book some more. Worked so well with Piper at the other desk, and we had a scotch at the end of the day. Worked till four. Worse than that, all day I wanted to cry, and tonight I did, with my French editor in the washroom, then I left the stage and went out back and the garden was lit up with torches. Would having a child prevent all this? Would rather sit and wonder. Write about people slowly, because people do move slowly. Write by hand. Write the book that—when a person is taking a thirteen-hour train to a city they're not sure they want to go to, to stay with a man they're not sure they can stay with, leaving behind their marriage on New Year's Day, nervous about having enticed a new man too much, and having listened to the mix tape made by their ex-husband, which is so heartbreaking, so now it's finally clear what he is feeling and the things he has been thinking, and her heart is aching, and maybe she will go back to him but she doesn't want to yet, and this lostness—this feeling like she just wants someone to take her heart in their hands and lay it in a bowl of warm blood and lap it in the blood with their hands, just wash their heart gently, polishing it like a pearl so it will come out thicker, shinier, and ready to be put back in the coffin of her chest, so she can step off the train like someone who's had a good upbringing and has been loved, who can look herself square in the eye without deceit, and can look everyone square in the eye without deceit, so they are understood by her and she by them, like a fresh rain and a sudden blooming—write the book that this person would choose. Write your book, you self-indulgent fool. Writing your damn books is the only thing that makes anything worthwhile.

Yes, I replied. Yes, I think love is important. Yes, neat fingers on those girls. Yes, purpose and meaning. Yes, she's so beautiful. Yes, the selling of one's soul. Yes, you do feel like you failed at something. Yesterday all I could think about was future suffering. Yesterday ended badly. Yesterday I bought a new bookshelf. Yesterday I bought him binoculars during a farcical adventure at one of the pawnshops down on Queen Street. Yesterday I bought myself a book on St. Petersburg, which I didn't want to read as soon I bought it. Yesterday I cried so much, never having cried so much about a break-up ever. Yesterday I did not sleep, and in the morning I put on some clothes and moved into the new hotel. Yesterday I dyed my hair red. Yesterday I felt so tired of the people around me, and again thought of escaping this place. Yesterday I got a library card. Yesterday I had a phone conversation. Yesterday I spent a long day at the printer's. Yesterday in the bathroom I had the feeling that I could not remember who was in my bed. Yesterday Lemons called to tell me he was single. Yesterday night I had the horrible feeling that New York had changed me for the worse and that everyone could see it. Yesterday night I was emailing with Pavel—more break-up stuff, it feels more real this time, more of a decision. Yesterday night was nice, he and I got drunk and looked in everyone's rooms. Yesterday she died. Yesterday there was a woman dancing at the bar, she was the only woman dancing. Yesterday was a good day until I checked my email, then my life suddenly became cluttered. Yesterday was Grandma's Shiva. Yesterday was the day I met that man, the divorce lawyer, on the streetcar. Yet I intend to go to California in the fall and sit on the beach and read all of Freud and finish my book. Yet if she didn't risk dying, could she be said to be truly living? Yet some part of me can compare. Yet some sudden, intimate life. Yet that is not enough. Yet we do love each other. Yet when I am in a dilemma now and I ask myself what to do, I feel I always come up with the right answer, the answer that will lead me in the direction of being a woman, which is where I want to go. You always telescope back into yourself and your own experiences, but how about telescoping out into the world? You always want to be working, which is

208

all right, too, but what about everything else in your life? You apply your love to a person for a long time and look at what happens. You are a new person now. You are able to be honest, and talk about problems. You are finding this gradual evolution and changing the most interesting thing about life, and where life truly lies, to see that there is forgiveness and things continue through time, and that there is strength in bonds which persist through so much, and when one thinks that one's relationships have completely been shattered, often they turn out unshattered and still to strongly exist. You are fine. You are just sitting here. You are not an example to anyone. You are nothing but slime, aspiring slime. You are wasting your life, always ruminating on men. You aren't the brains. You can change what you're doing and what you think you're doing, but first you must start by seeing what it is you are doing. You can feel sad about it. You can kill things. You can make all sorts of excuses, and contrive all sorts of clues to prove that he wants you, but they are just illusions. You can tell by looking at a woman's hand. You can't afford to move to New York. You can't grow if you are in a pot of concrete, and that's what Toronto is—a pot of concrete. You can't set out to do things as though life were a game. You can't sit back passively and expect fate to make things happen. *You deserve someone who is good for you in every way*, she said. You deserve to be happy. You did it, now move on. You do not run a blog. You do not work at a job. You don't have to be afraid and always anticipating. You don't have to correspond with everyone. You don't have to do anything you don't want to. You don't have to have your personality. You don't have to know your own worth. You don't have to make every decision, just a few. You don't have to threaten your own stability. You don't know where a situation is going to take you, or what element in any situation is going to be the most important one, or what function anything is going to serve, or what the results of anything will be. You don't need to come out ahead in anything. You don't need to explain your theories. You ended up where you began. You fantasising about the next stage of life is a way of avoiding the work of finishing the book that must be finished now. You forgot to wish for money, for health, for a robust sense of life; you only wished to write. You had one, one shot at a wish, one chance, and that was it. You have a home. You have a relationship. *You have been working hard*, he said. You have gotten into the social thicket, you've seen it. You have had so many opportunities to leave and you've never taken one. You have had twenty-seven years of evidence. *You have no instinctive insight into me*, I said. You have to battle and to enjoy the fight. You have to feel it and accept in your heart what you have been unable to accept from the very beginning—that he loves you. *You have to fuck people, you have to fuck everybody*, Claire said. You have to not write any more follow-up emails. You know you carry this weapon inside you, and that you are also a weapon. You know you look to men to distract you from your work. You like him about as much as you hate him. You like how he takes your head in his hands when he kisses you, and the feeling in your heart when you saw his gift, and how he said he wanted to learn how to sleep with you—that this was something he wanted to learn how to do. *You look confused*, I told him after he'd come, and he said, *don't I always look that way?* You must look at the books placed into your hands as masters to learn from still. You must wake up early. You need a new technique. You need so much stimulation to feel so little. You never wished to have fame, or a middle-class existence, or to be happily with one man forever. You plan for the future by how an imagined future makes you feel, yet you know that any future is unlikely to contain the elements you project onto it when you make your plans. You probably won't move to New York. You probably won't move to Paris. You see magic and beauty everywhere. You see the ants and the birds and the squirrels and the clouds—they also have no aim. You spent two months in Spain. You want to write, to do nothing but write? You will probably die in Toronto. You will see a few people, and that will be that. You would have attempted a conversation but you were too shy. You wouldn't dare try. You're killing me here. You're killing me. Your apprentice books. Your apprentice life. Your ugly hollow aspiration.

Zadie Smith's husband, who was my favourite person to talk to that night, said he thought a pet was a good release valve for the thoughts and feelings one could not share with one's partner.